Deutschland
Germany

Dr. Peter Albrecht

Deutschland
Germany

EDITION XXL

Inhalt
Contents

Schleswig-Holstein 10

Mecklenburg-Vorpommern 18

Hamburg 28

Freie Hansestadt Bremen 34

Brandenburg 40

Niedersachsen 50

Berlin 60

Sachsen-Anhalt 74

Nordrhein-Westfalen 82

Sachsen 92

Thüringen 104

Hessen 114

Rheinland-Pfalz 126

Saarland 138

Baden-Württemberg 144

Bayern 154

Schleswig-Holstein *10*

Mecklenburg-Lower Pomerania *18*

Hamburg *28*

Free Hanseatic City of Bremen *34*

Brandenburg *40*

Lower Saxony *50*

Berlin *60*

Saxony-Anhalt *74*

North Rhine-Westphalia *82*

Saxony *92*

Thuringia *104*

Hesse *114*

Rhineland-Palatinate *126*

Saarland *138*

Baden-Wurttemberg *144*

Bavaria *154*

Vorwort
Foreword

━ Verglichen mit anderen Ländern der Erde ist Deutschland ein relativ kleines Land. Mit modernen Verkehrsmitteln kann Deutschland innerhalb weniger Stunden durchquert werden. Angenommen, Sie würden dies tun, dann könnten Sie in rascher Folge die unterschiedlichsten landschaftlichen und kulturellen Regionen erleben. Deutschland ist außerordentlich vielfältig.

Aus diesem Grund sollten Sie Deutschland besser nicht durcheilen. Deutschland ist es wert, dass Sie sich Zeit nehmen, das Land zu erkunden. Ob Sie weite Meeresstrände im Norden, bergige Alpenregionen oder sonnige Weinberge vorziehen: Sie werden immer ein lohnendes Ziel finden. Es wäre schön, wenn dieses Buch Ihnen dabei behilflich sein könnte.

▓ Compared with many other countries on this planet, Germany is relatively small. Taking modern means of transport, you may cross Germany within a few hours. Supposed you did so, you would experience a rapid change of very different landscapes and cultural regions. Germany is extraordinarily varied.

This is why you should not hurry through Germany. It is worth taking time for Germany and to explore the country. Whether you prefer wide sandy beaches, mountain areas in the Alps or sunny vineyards: You will always find a goal worth seeing. It would be perfect if this book could assist you in your planning.

9

Schleswig-Holstein
Schleswig-Holstein

Die traumhafte Küste von Westerhever
bei St. Peter-Ording in Nordfriesland mit
ihrem bekannten Leuchtturm.

*The fantastic coast of Westerhever near
St. Peter-Ording, North Frisia, with its
well known lighthouse.*

10

Lage:	nördlichstes Bundesland Deutschlands
Fläche:	15 763 km²
Einwohner:	2,8 Millionen
Landeshauptstadt:	Kiel
Inseln:	7
Küstenlänge:	1190 km
Position:	*most northern state of the Federal Republic of Germany*
Area:	*6,086 sq miles*
Inhabitants:	*2.8 million*
Capital:	*Kiel*
Islands:	*7*
Length of Coast:	*740 miles*

Schleswig-Holstein, das „Land zwischen den Meeren", zwischen Nordsee und Ostsee, gehört zu den beliebtesten Urlaubsregionen Deutschlands. 4,5 Millionen Gäste besuchen jedes Jahr die Seebäder und Inseln, genießen die unendlichen Sandstrände, den Wind und die Wellen. Ein einmaliges Naturerlebnis an der Nordseeküste bietet das Schleswig-Holsteinische Wattenmeer, der größte Nationalpark in Mitteleuropa: die Wattwanderung bei Ebbe – natürlich nur unter ortskundiger Führung.

An der Ostseeküste laden die Landeshauptstadt Kiel und die historische Hansestadt Lübeck zu Sport und Kultur ein. Die „Kieler Woche", das vielleicht größte und berühmteste Segelsport-Fest, findet jährlich im Frühsommer statt.

Schleswig-Holstein, the land between the North Sea and the Baltic Sea, is one of the most popular holiday regions of Germany. 4.5 million guests visit the seaside resorts as well as the islands every year. They enjoy the never ending sandy beaches, the wind and the waves. The "Watt" coastline of Schleswig-Holstein, which represents the largest national park in central Europe, offers the unique experience of guided tours through the mud flats.

The capital Kiel at the Baltic coast and the historical city of Lübeck attract with sports and culture. The "Kieler Woche" is probably the largest and most famous sailing festival taking place every year in June.

Kiel
Kiel

Landeshauptstadt von Schleswig-Holstein	
Fläche:	120 km²
Einwohner:	230 000
Capital of Schleswig-Holstein	
Area:	*46 sq miles*
Inhabitants:	*230,000*

► Kiel ist der Heimathafen der Gorch Fock, dem bekanntesten Schulschiff der deutschen Marine.

 ► *Kiel is the home port of the windjammer Gorch Fock which is the best known training ship of the German navy.*

◄ Blick über die Strandkörbe von Laboe zu den Kitesurfern auf der Kieler Förde.

◄ *View from the beach chairs of Laboe to the kitesurfers on the Firth of Kiel.*

🇩🇪 Über viele Jahrhunderte war Kiel eine relativ kleine Stadt mit weniger als 20 000 Einwohnern. Erst nach 1864, nachdem Kiel preußischer Kriegshafen wurde, begann ein rasantes Wachstum zum heute wichtigsten Ostseehafen Schleswig-Holsteins.

Die Nähe zum Meer prägt die gesamte Stadt. Von hier aus starten die großen Fährschiffe nach Skandinavien. Eine Hafenrundfahrt sollte immer im Besuchsprogramm enthalten sein. Sehenswert sind auch die Schleusenanlagen am Endpunkt des Nord-Ostsee-Kanals in Kiel-Holtenau.

1972 wurden in Kiel die olympischen Segelregatten ausgetragen. Eine der größten segelsportlichen Veranstaltungen der Welt ist die Kieler Woche, an der jährlich Tausende von Segelbooten aus allen Kontinenten teilnehmen. Einen Höhepunkt der Kieler Woche bildet eine große Windjammerparade auf der Kieler Förde, oft angeführt von der Gorch Fock.

🇬🇧 *For many hundreds of years, Kiel was a relatively small town with less than 20,000 inhabitants. Only after 1864, when Kiel became a Prussian naval harbour, the city grew up rapidly into the most important Baltic port of Schleswig-Holstein by now.*

From here, the ferries leave for Scandinavia. A boat trip around the harbour should always be a part of the visitor's program, as well as the locks at the end of the Kiel Canal in Kiel-Holtenau.

In 1972, the Olympic Sailing Regatta took place at the coast of Kiel. One of the world's greatest sailing events is the yearly "Kieler Woche" with thousands of boats from all over the world. A special highlight is the windjammers parade on the Firth of Kiel with the old Gorch Fock usually ahead of all of them.

▼ Laboe an der Kieler Förde

13

▼ *The village of Laboe on the banks of the Firth of Kiel*

Insel Sylt
Sylt Island

Sylt ist mit fast 100 km² Fläche die größte Nordseeinsel Deutschlands. Zur offenen Nordsee hin erstreckt sich ein 40 km langer Sandstrand. Das Klima wird durch den Golfstrom beeinflusst und ist sehr mild. Die mittlere jährliche Sonnenscheindauer ist länger als auf dem benachbarten Festland. Die größte Stadt auf Sylt, Westerland, gehört daher zu den beliebtesten Heilbädern in Deutschland.

With an area of about 40 sq miles, the island of Sylt is the largest of all German North Sea islands. Towards the open sea there are 25 miles of sandy beaches. Thanks to the Gulf Stream the climate is relatively mild. The average sunshine hours per year are above those of the mainland next to the island. Due to that Westerland, the largest town on the island, is one of the most popular spas in Germany.

▲ Der Leuchtturm Westellenbogen am Nordende von Sylt wurde 1852 erbaut und ist Deutschlands ältester eiserner Leuchtturm.

▲ *The lighthouse Westellenbogen at the northern end of Sylt built in 1852 is Germany's oldest iron lighthouse.*

14

▲ Weite Dünengebiete und die breitesten Sandstrände Nordeuropas beherrschen das Bild von Amrum. Die höchste Düne ist 32 m hoch.

▲ *Large areas of sand dunes and the widest sandy beaches of Northern Europe are typical for Amrum. The largest dune is 100 feet in height.*

Insel Amrum
Amrum Island

Amrum gehört zu den Nordfriesischen Inseln und liegt südlich von Sylt. Zwischen der Insel und dem Festland breitet sich das Wattenmeer aus. Bei Niedrigwasser kann man die Nachbarinsel Föhr per Wattwanderung erreichen. Nach Amrum gelangt man mit einer der Fähren von Sylt oder vom Festland aus. Auf der Insel ist das Fahrrad das bevorzugte Verkehrsmittel.

Amrum is a part of the North Frisian Islands south of Sylt. The widespread Watt landscape between the island and the mainland allows walking to the neighbouring island Föhr at low tide. Amrum may be reached either by ferry from Sylt or from the mainland. The usual vehicle on Amrum, however, is the bicycle.

Flensburg
Flensburg

Die nördlichste Stadt Deutschlands liegt unmittelbar an der deutsch-dänischen Grenze. Historisch ist Flensburg eng mit Dänemark verbunden. Es stand 400 Jahre lang unter der dänischen Krone. Aus den dänischen Kolonien in der Karibik wurde bis ins 19. Jahrhundert Zuckerrohr importiert und in Flensburg raffiniert.

Die gut erhaltene Altstadt mit ihren berühmten Kapitäns- und Kaufmannshöfen lädt zu endlosen Entdeckungsreisen ein. Viele kleine Geschäfte mit allerlei Spezialitäten und Antiquitäten lassen Flensburg zu „der" Einkaufsstadt zwischen Hamburg und Kopenhagen werden.

Zu einem maritimen Volksfest hat sich in den letzten Jahren die „Rum-Regatta" auf der Flensburger Innenförde entwickelt. Rum war viele Jahre das wichtigste Handelsgut der Stadt. Zur Erinnerung treffen sich jährlich Ende Mai weit über 100 traditionelle Gaffelsegler zur Regatta. Der zweite Platz wird mit einer großen Flasche Rum belohnt.

Nearest to Denmark, Flensburg is the most northerly town of Germany. Flensburg used to belong to the Kingdom of Denmark for about 400 years. Up to the 19th century, Flensburg imported sugar cane from the Caribbean colonies of Denmark. The refining of the sugar was done in Flensburg.

The historical city with famous buildings of former traders and captains invites one to make endless discoveries. Many small shops offer all kinds of specialities and antiques which make Flensburg "the" shopping place between Hamburg and Copenhagen.

In recent years, a maritime public festival, the so-called "Rum Regatta", has been re-established on the Firth of Flensburg. For many years, rum was the most important commodity of the city. As a memory, more than 100 traditional gaffyachts meet every year end of May for a regatta. Not the very best, but the second best wins a large bottle of rum.

❚ Für viele Segler ist der Flensburger Segelhafen der schönste Hafen überhaupt.

❚ *For many sailors, the yacht harbour of Flensburg is the most beautiful port of all.*

15

Lübeck
Lübeck

▬ Lübeck ist eine der traditionsreichsten Hansestädte und verfügt über den größten deutschen Ostseehafen. Von hier aus ist der gesamte Ostseeraum, insbesondere auch das Baltikum, erreichbar. Die mittelalterliche Altstadt liegt zum größten Teil auf einer Insel zwischen Trave und Wakenitz und ist – zusammen mit weiteren Bauwerken Lübecks sind es über 1000 Gebäude – Teil des UNESCO-Welterbes.

Zur Literaturstadt wurde Lübeck durch die Schriftstellerbrüder Thomas Mann und Heinrich Mann. Das Buddenbrookhaus in der Mengstraße neben der Lübecker Marienkirche gilt als „Geburtshaus" der bekannten Literatur. Beinahe schon weltweite Berühmtheit hat das Lübecker Marzipan, das seit dem späten Mittelalter in Lübeck hergestellt wird.

Ein bedeutender Stadtteil von Lübeck ist das traditionsreiche (seit 1802) und elegante Seebad Travemünde. Im Hafen von Travemünde liegt unter anderem ein ehemaliges Segelschulschiff, die berühmte Viermastbark Passat, als Museumsschiff und Wahrzeichen.

❚ Das Holstentor gilt als Wahrzeichen der Hansestadt Lübeck. Es gehörte zur ehemaligen Befestigungsanlage und grenzte die Innenstadt nach Westen ab.

❚ *The Holstentor is a symbol of Lübeck. It was a part of a former fortress and was the west gate of the historical town center.*

▦ *Lübeck is one of the traditional members of the German Hanseatic League and has the largest Baltic port of Germany. The whole Baltic area can be reached from Lübeck. The major part of the medieval centre is located on an island between the rivers Trave and Wakenitz. It is a UNESCO cultural world heritage site which includes altogether more than 1,000 buildings.*

Furthermore, Lübeck is well known as a city of literature. The writers and brothers Thomas Mann and Heinrich Mann lived there. Their "House of Buddenbrooks", Mengstraße, close to St. Mary's Church (Marienkirche), is said to be the birthplace of the Nobel-prize winning literature. A very famous present from Lübeck is marzipan, which has been produced here since the Middle Ages.

An important part of Lübeck is the tradition-rich high society seaside resort Travemünde. A former training sailing ship, the famous four-master Passat, can be visited in the harbour of Travemünde.

▲ Gelb blühende Rapsfelder in der
Holsteinischen Schweiz

▲ *Yellow blooming rape fields in
Holstein's Switzerland*

Holsteinische Schweiz
Holstein's Switzerland

▬ Zwischen Kiel im Norden und Lübeck im Süden erstreckt sich der größte Naturpark Schleswig-Holsteins, die Holsteinische Schweiz. Wer mit dem Namen Schweiz die Attribute „herrliche, hügelige Landschaft" und „solider Wohlstand" in Verbindung bringt, der kann sich die Holsteinische Schweiz schon recht gut vorstellen.

Die nährstoffreichen Böden gestatten seit Jahrhunderten eine intensive landwirtschaftliche Nutzung, in deren Gefolge prächtige Besitztümer – Gutshäuser und Schlösser des Landadels – entstanden.

Die abwechslungsreiche Landschaft der Holsteinischen Schweiz bietet zahlreiche Möglichkeiten zu aktivem Urlaub. Der Naturparkweg verbindet auf einer Gesamtlänge von 117 km die fünf Naturparks in Schleswig-Holstein. Die zahlreichen Seen, allen voran der Große Plöner See und seine angrenzenden Nachbar-Seen, erfreuen sich unter Wassersportlern und Anglern großer Beliebtheit.

🇬🇧 *Between Kiel in the north and Lübeck in the south Holstein's Switzerland which is the largest natural park of Schleswig-Holstein is expanding. Associating Switzerland with lovely hills and healthy prosperity helps to imagine what Holstein's Switzerland really is.*

The high-nutrient soil has for centuries allowed intensive agricultural usage. The rich country enabled great estates and castles of the landed gentry to be established.

The varied landscape of Holstein's Switzerland offers a lot of possibilities for active holidays. The "Naturparkweg" is a track of 73 miles which leads through five natural parks of Holstein's Switzerland. A number of lakes, especially the lake "Großer Plöner See" and some lakes in the neighbourhood are very popular fishing and sporting areas.

Mecklenburg-Vorpommern
Mecklenburg-Lower Pomerania

Landschaft bei Alt auf der Insel Rügen

Island Rügen close to the village of Alt

18

Lage:	nördliches Bundesland an der Ostsee
Fläche:	23 200 km²
Einwohner:	1,7 Millionen
Landeshauptstadt:	Schwerin
Küstenlänge:	1700 km
Position:	*northern state at the Baltic Sea*
Area:	*8960 sq miles*
Inhabitants:	*1.7 million*
Capital:	*Schwerin*
Length of Coast:	*1056 miles*

Schwerin

▬ Mecklenburg-Vorpommern ist das am dünnsten besiedelte deutsche Bundesland. Gleichzeitig hat die geschützte Natur den höchsten Flächenanteil: Mehr als ein Viertel der Landesfläche stehen unter Natur- oder Landschaftsschutz. Wer im Urlaub Ruhe genießen will, ist in Mecklenburg-Vorpommern gut aufgehoben. Mit 7,6 Millionen Touristen zählte das Land im vergangenen Jahr vier Mal mehr Gäste als Einwohner.

Wollte man alle weißen Sandstrände einschließlich der Inseln ablaufen, hätte man einen Fußmarsch von 1700 km vor sich. Lange Spaziergänge unternahm auch der berühmteste Maler des Landes, Caspar David Friedrich (1774–1840), der in seinen Werken wie „Kreidefelsen auf Rügen" die Natur romantisch exakt festhielt.

🇬🇧 *Mecklenburg-Lower Pomerania is the most sparsely populated state of Germany. At the same time, nature conservancy occupies the highest share of the area. More than one quarter of the land has been declared a protected area. Mecklenburg-Lower Pomerania is a good place for holiday-makers who want to enjoy peace and quiet. Last year, the state welcomed 7.6 million visitors – four times more visitors than inhabitants.*

A walk along all the white sandy beaches, inclusive the islands, would mean more than 1,000 miles. A famous walker and romantic artist was Caspar David Friedrich (1774–1840), who painted, besides others, the "Chalk Cliffs of Rügen".

19

20

Schwerin
Schwerin

Landeshauptstadt von Mecklenburg-Vorpommern	
Fläche:	130 km²
Einwohner:	98 000
Capital of Mecklenburg-Lower Pomerania	
Area:	*50 sq miles*
Inhabitants:	*98,000*

► Ein 1837 geplantes herzogliches Palais beherbergt das Staatliche Museum.

► *A ducal palace designed in 1837 houses the state museum.*

◄ Das Schweriner Schloss auf einer
Insel im Schweriner See ist heute Sitz
des Landesparlaments.

◄ *The palace of Schwerin on an island of
the Lake Schwerin is now the residence
of the Mecklenburg-Lower Pomerania
parliament.*

▬ Schwerin ist die kleinste deutsche Landeshauptstadt. An der Stelle des heutigen Schlosses
stand bereits im 10. Jahrhundert eine Burg, in
deren unmittelbarer Umgebung sich die Stadt entwickelte. Das Schloss war in der Vergangenheit Residenz mecklenburgischer Herzöge und ist heute
Sitz des mecklenburg-vorpommerschen Landtages.

In den Jahren ab 1991 unternahm Schwerin große
Anstrengungen, den historischen Stadtkern zu
sanieren, was im bundesweiten Wettbewerb zur
„Erhaltung des Historischen Stadtraumes in den
neuen Bundesländern 1992–1994" mit der Gold-
plakette gewürdigt wurde.

Das Stadtgebiet von Schwerin umfasst zwölf Seen,
auf denen beste Bedingungen für den Wassersport
gegeben sind. Insbesondere auf dem größten der
Seen, dem Schweriner See, werden vereinsmäßig
Segeln und Rudern betrieben.

🇬🇧 *Schwerin is the smallest capital city of
a German state. The predecessor of the
present palace was a 10th century fortress
which became the centre of the developing
town. In the past, the palace was a residence of the Dukes of Mecklenburg. Today,
it houses the parliament of Mecklenburg-
Lower Pomerania.*

*From 1991, Schwerin made huge efforts
to reconstruct the historical town centre.
As a result, it received a gold medal as the
winner of the Federal contest "Preserva-
tion of Historical Town Centres in the New
Federal States 1992–1994".*

*Twelve lakes within the Schwerin city area
offer best conditions for water sports. Especially the lake "Schweriner See", the
largest one, is a very popular sailing and
rowing area.*

21

Wismar
Wismar

▬ Die Stadt Wismar wurde im frühen
13. Jahrhundert an der Stelle eines natürlichen Ostseehafens gegründet. Noch im selben Jahrhundert wurde Wismar Mitglied
der Hanse und erlangte als Handelshafen an
der „Hanseatischen Ostseestraße" im Mittelalter große Bedeutung.

Ab 1991 wurde der historische Stadtkern
gründlich saniert. Wismar ist die einzige in
voller Größe und Geschlossenheit erhaltene
mittelalterliche Hansestadt im Ostseeraum
und bietet das authentische Bild einer damaligen Seehandelsstadt. Seit dem Jahr 2002 ist
Wismars Altstadt UNESCO-Weltkulturerbe.

🇬🇧 *The town of Wismar was founded in the 13th century at a place where
the Baltic Sea formed a natural port. Also in the course of this century, Wismar became a member of the Hanseatic League and became an important
trading port at the "Hanseatic Baltic Sea Route" during the Middle Ages.*

*From 1991, the historical town centre was extensively renovated. Wismar
is the only completely preserved Baltic Hanseatic town from the Middle
Ages and it offers an authentic picture of a former trading port. In 2002,
Wismar became a UNESCO World Heritage Site.*

► Die St.-Nikolai-Kirche war die Kirche
der Seefahrer und Fischer.

► *The church St Nikolai was the home
church of sailors and fishermen.*

Rostock
Rostock

Rostock liegt an der Ostsee, dort, wo die Mündung des Flusses Warnow einen großen natürlichen Hafen bildet. Seit dem 13. Jahrhundert war Rostock Mitglied der Hanse und wurde zum wichtigsten Hafen in Mecklenburg. Die im Jahr 1419 gegründete Universität Rostock, die bis heute ohne Unterbrechung ihre Lehrtätigkeit ausübt, gehört zu den ältesten Universitäten Nordeuropas.

Rostock besitzt heute im Stadtteil Warnemünde den größten deutschen Kreuzfahrthafen, was nicht zuletzt der guten Verkehrsanbindung an den Raum Berlin zu verdanken ist. Das Ostseebad Warnemünde verfügt über einen 150 m breiten Sandstrand.

Einen Besuch wert ist der Rostocker Zoo, der sich schwerpunktmäßig mit der Haltung und der Zucht von Tieren des arktischen Lebensraumes beschäftigt.

The Baltic Sea town of Rostock is located at a place where the estuary of the river Warnow forms a large natural port. From the 13th century, Rostock was a member of the Hanseatic League and became the most important port of Mecklenburg. The University of Rostock was founded in 1419 and is one of the oldest universities in northern Europe.

Warnemünde, which is a district of Rostock, has the largest German port for cruise ships. The seaside resort Warnemünde offers a sandy beach which is up to 500 feet wide.

The Rostock zoo is also worth visiting. It mainly concentrates on breeding animals of the arctic habitat.

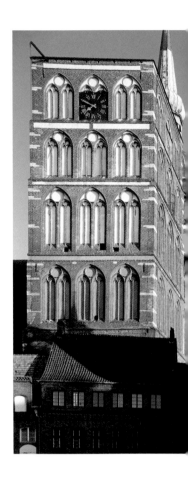

▼ Der Neue Markt in Rostock mit der Marienkirche im Hintergrund.

▼ *The Rostock square Neuer Markt with the church St. Maria in the background.*

Stralsund
Stralsund

■ Die Hansestadt Stralsund wird auch als Tor zur Insel Rügen bezeichnet – und für Auto- und Bahnfahrer ist sie es auch tatsächlich. Die hervorragend sanierte Altstadt Stralsunds gehört seit dem Jahr 2002 zum UNESCO-Weltkulturerbe. Mit dem Deutschen Meeresmuseum, das Einblicke in die Welt des Wassers bietet, besitzt Stralsund das meistbesuchte Museum Norddeutschlands.

⬛ *The Hanseatic town of Stralsund is called the gate to the island of Rügen. And indeed, it is the gate for trains and car drivers. The excellent renovated old town centre of Stralsund became a UNESCO World Heritage Site in 2002. The "Deutsches Meeresmuseum" is the best visited museum in northern Germany. It allows an impressive look into the world of water.*

◄ Der Bau des Rathauses von Stralsund wurde im 13. Jahrhundert begonnen.

◄ *The town hall of Stralsund was founded in the 13th century.*

23

Insel Hiddensee
Hiddensee Island

■ Westlich von Rügen in der Ostsee liegt Hiddensee, eine fast 17 km lange, aber streckenweise nur wenige hundert Meter breite Insel. Die jährliche Sonnenscheindauer ist auf der Insel deutlich länger als auf dem Festland. Daher war Hiddensee als „Insel des Lichts" schon immer ein beliebtes Ziel von Malern. Aber auch die kulinarischen Spezialitäten der Insel locken viele Gäste an.

⬛ *The Baltic Sea Island Hiddensee, west of Rügen, is a small island which is nearly 10 miles long but partly only a few hundred metres in wide. The average sunshine hours per year are far above those on the mainland. This is why Hiddensee – being called the "island of light" – has always been a popular working place for painters. The island is also attractive because of its culinary specialities.*

▲ Der Leuchtturm „Dornbusch" von 1888 ist das Wahrzeichen der Insel Hiddensee. Er bietet einen großartigen Blick über die Insel.

▲ *The lighthouse "Dornbusch" from 1888 is the symbol of Hiddensee Island. It offers a great view over the island.*

Deutsche Alleenstraße
German Avenue Route

▬ Die Deutsche Alleenstraße zieht sich als 2500 km langes grünes Band durch ganz Deutschland. Sie beginnt im Norden auf der Insel Rügen und endet im Süden auf der Insel Reichenau im Bodensee. Dazwischen passiert sie die ausgedehnten Seenlandschaften in Mecklenburg-Vorpommern, einige Mittelgebirge, das Rheinland und den Schwarzwald. Insgesamt führt sie durch acht Bundesländer.

🇬🇧 *The "German Avenue Route" is a 1,550 mile long green avenue across Germany. It starts in the north on the island of Rügen and ends up in the south on the island of Reichenau in Lake Constance (Bodensee). In between the avenue passes the extensive countryside of Mecklenburg-Lower Pomerania which is rich in lakes, some low mountain ranges, the Rhineland as well as the Black Forest. The whole avenue crosses eight states.*

► In ihrem ursprünglichen Zustand gut erhaltene Alleen mit dichten, grünen Laubdächern findet man noch in Mecklenburg-Vorpommern.

► *Well preserved avenues with dense green roofs of foliage can still be found in Mecklenburg-Lower Pomerania.*

24

Insel Rügen
Island of Rügen

▬ Rügen ist die größte deutsche Insel. Der Rügendamm verbindet die Insel mit der Hansestadt Stralsund auf dem Festland. Durch zahlreiche Meeresbuchten und Landzungen erreicht die Küste Rügens eine Gesamtlänge von 574 km. Die traditionsreichen Seebäder Binz, Sellin und Göhren gehören zu den beliebtesten Ferienorten auf Rügen. Die Insel lässt sich bestens mit dem Fahrrad oder auch mit dem Segelboot erkunden.

🇬🇧 *The island of Rügen is the largest German island. The Rügen causeway serves as a connection with the Hanseatic Stralsund on the mainland. Due to numerous bays and promontories, the total length of the Rügen coastline adds up to almost 360 miles. The traditional sea resorts Binz, Sellin and Göhren are among the most popular places for holiday-makers. The island can be best explored by bicycle or by sailing.*

◄ Die schneeweißen Kreidefelsen zählen zu den klassischen Sehenswürdigkeiten der Insel Rügen.

◄ *The snow white chalk cliffs belong to the classic sights of the island of Rügen.*

Insel Usedom
Usedom Island

▬ Usedom ist die östlichste deutsche Insel – ein Fünftel der Insel gehört bereits zu Polen. Die Insel ist vom deutschen Festland aus über zwei Brücken erreichbar. Auf Usedom verbindet die Usedomer Bäderbahn die Ostseebäder an der nordöstlichen Küste. Im Norden befindet sich in Peenemünde ein „historisch-technisches Informationszentrum der Raumfahrt".

⊞ *Usedom is the most eastern German island – one fifth of the island belongs to Poland. From the German mainland, the island is accessible via two bridges. On the island, the Usedom resort railway links the sea resorts at the north-eastern coast. Peenemünde in the north of the island has a historical-technical space travel information centre.*

▼ Ahlbeck auf der Insel Usedom ist das östlichste Seebad Deutschlands.

▼ *Ahlbeck on Usedom Island is the easternmost see resort of Germany.*

Neubrandenburg
Neubrandenburg

Neubrandenburg liegt im Südosten Mecklenburgs, etwa in der Mitte zwischen Berlin und der Insel Rügen. Die Gründung der Stadt lässt sich exakt datieren: Sie erfolgte am 4. Januar 1248 durch Markgraf Johann I. von Brandenburg. Im frühen 14. Jahrhundert wurde die Stadt mit steinernen Stadtmauern und drei, später vier Stadttoren befestigt. Stadtmauer und Stadttore sind mitsamt ihren Türmen und Wachhäusern vollständig erhalten. Neubrandenburg wird heute noch die „Stadt der vier Tore" genannt.

Die Konzertkirche St. Marien bietet den Musikfreunden ein anspruchsvolles Programm. Die Kirche ist Heimstatt der Neubrandenburger Philharmonie und Veranstaltungsort der Festspiele Mecklenburg-Vorpommern.

Neubrandenburg liegt direkt am Tollensesee, der mit 11 km Länge und fast 3 km Breite Spaziergänger, Badelustige und Wassersportler anzieht. Um den See führt ein 37 km langer Radwanderweg – genau das Richtige für einen gemütlichen Tagesausflug mit der Familie.

Neubrandenburg is a town in the south-east of Mecklenburg, north of Berlin. The foundation of the town can be exactly fixed as on January 4, 1248, by Margrave John I of Brandenburg. During the early 14th century, the town was fortified with stone walls and three – later four – town gates. The wall and the gates are still complete today, inclusive their Wachhäuser (guardrooms), and are in excellent condition. Neubrandenburg is still called "the town of the four gates".

The medieval church Marienkirche is now restored as a concert hall. It houses the Neubrandenburg Philharmonic Orchestra and is the location of the Mecklenburg-Lower Pomerania festivals.

Neubrandenburg is located close to the lake Tollense, which is seven miles in length and two miles in width. The lake is popular with walkers, swimmers and water sportsmen. A 23 mile long bicycle route around the lake is perfect for one day family trips.

▼ Das Stargarder Tor von 1350, eines der schönsten Gotik-Gebäude Norddeutschlands, war Teil der Stadtmauer.

▼ *The Stargader Tor from 1350, one of the most beautiful gothic buildings in Northern Germany, was a part of the town wall.*

27

▲ Der historische Altstadtkern von Röbel
liegt direkt am Ufer des Müritzsees.

▲ *The historical town centre of Röbel is
directly at the shore of the lake Müitz.*

Müritz
Lake Müritz

▬ Die Müritz ist ein See innerhalb der Mecklen-
burgischen Seenplatte, und zwar nach dem Bodensee der zweitgrößte See Deutschlands mit einer
Nord-Süd-Ausdehnung von 29 km. Allerdings ist die
Müritz sehr flach: Die Tiefe beträgt im Durchschnitt
nur 6 m. Die Müritz ist wie die gesamte Mecklen-
burgische Seenplatte ein ideales Revier für Sport-
boote. Mit gemieteten Segel- oder Motorjachten,
auf denen man auch bequem wohnen kann, lässt
sich die gesamte Region vom Wasser aus erkunden.

Die größte Stadt an der Müritz ist der Luftkurort
Waren (Müritz) am Nordende des Sees. Der Ort
wurde bereits vor nahezu 2000 Jahren als Siedlungs-
platz urkundlich erwähnt. Der schöne, sehenswerte
Stadthafen von Waren (Müritz) hatte in den 20er-
Jahren des vorigen Jahrhunderts erhebliche wirtschaftliche Bedeutung für die Stadt.

▨ *The Müritz is a lake of the Mecklenburg lowland plain full of
lakes. It is the second largest German lake after Lake Constance.
From the north to the south the Müritz stretches for about 20 miles.
However, the Müritz is very shallow: less than 20 feet in the average. Like the whole Mecklenburg Lake District, the Müritz is an
ideal area for boats. Sailing yachts or motor yachts with comfort-
able accomodation may be chartered in order to explore the region
from the water.*

*The largest town at the Müritz is Waren (Müritz), a resort at the
northern shore of the lake. People settled here already 2000 years
ago. In the 1920s, the beautiful and interesting port of the town
was of great economic importance for Waren (Müritz).*

Hamburg
Hamburg

Blick auf die Außenalster und eine der be-
vorzugtesten Wohngegenden Hamburgs

*View to the lake Außenalster, surrounded
by one of the most preferred residential
areas of Hamburg*

28

Lage:	Tor zur Nordsee, von der Elbemündung 110 km stromaufwärts
Fläche:	755 km²
Einwohner:	1,8 Millionen
Landeshauptstadt:	Hamburg
Position:	*gate for the North Sea, 70 miles from the mouth of the Elbe*
Area:	*292 sq miles*
Inhabitants:	*1.8 million*
Capital:	*Hamburg*

▬ Hamburg, die zweitgrößte Stadt Deutschlands, ist ein Stadtstaat, der politisch einem Bundesland gleichgestellt ist. Der riesige Hafen, in dem die größten Überseeschiffe anlegen, hat Hamburg den Beinamen „Tor zur Welt" eingebracht. Die wirtschaftliche Bedeutung Hamburgs für den Außenhandel der Bundesrepublik Deutschland kommt auch darin zum Ausdruck, dass in Hamburg mehr als 100 Konsulate vertreten sind – mehr als in jeder anderen Stadt der Welt, abgesehen von Hongkong.

Eine weitere Superlative stellen die mehr als 2500 Brücken dar, welche die zahlreichen Flussarme und Kanäle überspannen. Die Hansestadt Hamburg ist die brückenreichste Stadt Europas. Zum Vergleich: Venedig besitzt 400 Brücken.

⌗ *Hamburg is the second largest city of Germany. It is a citystate with the same political standing as all other states of the Federal Republic. The huge port with the largest overseas ships gave Hamburg the name "gate to the world". Hamburg's economic importance for the German export results in more than 100 consulates, which is more than in any other city of the world except for Hong Kong, being located here.*

Another remarkable thing is the more than 2,500 bridges across the numerous arms of rivers and canals. No other city in Europe has more bridges than Hamburg. For instance: Venice has 400 bridges.

Hamburg
Hamburg

► Das Rathaus von Hamburg, der Sitz des Parlaments, wurde auf 4000 Eichenpfählen errichtet.

► *The city hall of Hamburg, the seat of the Hamburg parliament, is built on 4,000 stilts from oak.*

Binnen- und Außenalster
Lakes Binnen- and Außenalster

■ Die Alster ist ein Nebenfluss der Elbe. Bereits vor rund 800 Jahren wurde die Alster kurz vor ihrer Mündung in die Elbe in Hamburg aufgestaut, um Mühlen zu betreiben. Es entstand der Alstersee, der später durch einen Damm und Brücken geteilt wurde. Der kleinere Teilsee, die so genannte Binnenalster, liegt heute im Zentrum von Hamburg. Direkt an die Binnenalster grenzen das Hamburger Rathaus sowie moderne Geschäfts- und Kaufhäuser.

Der größere Teil des Alstersees, die Außenalster, ist von Grünflächen umgeben und wird viel für den Wassersport – Rudern und Segeln – genutzt. Am Ufer entlang führen rund 7 km Rad- und Wanderwege. Die unmittelbare Umgebung der Außenalster gehört zu den begehrtesten Wohnlagen Hamburgs.

◄ Der Rundweg um die Außenalster beträgt etwa 7 km.

◄ *The circular walk around the Außen- alster is about 5 miles.*

🇬🇧 *The river Alster is a tributary of the river Elbe. 800 years ago, the Alster was dammed in order to drive mills just before joining the Elbe. In this way the lake Alster was created. In later years, the lake was divided into a smaller lake called Binnenalster and a larger lake called Außenalster. The Binnenalster is today in the middle of the city. Elegant and modern business buildings and warehouses as well as the Hamburg City Hall are next to the Binnenalster.*

The lake Außenalster is surrounded by green parks and is used for water sports, mainly sailing and rowing. Along the shore there are about 5 miles of walking and bicycle routes. The Außenalster region is one of the most preferred residential areas of Hamburg.

▼ Die Binnenalster liegt direkt im Zentrum von Hamburg.

▼ *The lake Binnenalster is located in the centre of the city of Hamburg.*

Hamburger Hafen
The Port of Hamburg

Der Hamburger Hafen ist der größte Seehafen des Kontinents. Als Umschlagplatz für Rohkaffee ist er sogar die Nummer Eins in der Welt. Im gesamten Hafenbereich sind 50 000 Menschen beschäftigt. Die große Entfernung des Hafens von der offenen Nordsee – 110 km von der Elbe-Mündung – hat Vor- und Nachteile. Zu den Vorteilen gehören die relativ niedrigen Transportkosten, zu denen die Güter weit ins Landesinnere anstatt nur an die Küste gebracht werden.

Für Touristen sind die Sankt-Pauli-Landungsbrücken der vielleicht wichtigste Teil des Hamburger Hafens. Während früher hier die großen Übersee-Passagierdampfer anlegten, sind es heute vor allem Hafenrundfahrtschiffe und Fähren, unter anderem nach Helgoland. S-Bahn- und U-Bahn-Stationen machen die Sankt-Pauli-Landungsbrücken zu einem zentralen Verkehrsknotenpunkt in Hamburg.

The Port of Hamburg is the largest seaport on the European continent. As a trade centre for raw coffee beans it is even the world's number one port. About 50,000 people are employed in the complete harbour area. The large distance to the North Sea – 68 miles to the mouth of the river Elbe – has advantages as well as disadvantages. The goods can be carried into the interior rather than to the coast only – at low transportation costs.

Tourists may regard the "Sankt-Pauli-Landungsbrücken" (landing stages) as the most important part of the port, where in former days the big overseas passenger steamers landed. Today, boat trips round the port start from here as well as ferries, among others, the ferries for the island of Helgoland. Sankt-Pauli-Landungsbrücken is also a Hamburg traffic junction with railway (S-Bahn) and underground railway (U-Bahn) stations.

Speicherhäuser an einem der Hafenkanäle

Storehouses along one of the ports canals

Fischmarkt
Fish Market

🇩🇪 Um der Hansestadt Hamburg Konkurrenz zu machen, erhielt die damals dänisch beeinflusste Stadt Altona 1703 das Recht, sonntags vor dem Kirchgang Handel zu treiben. Seitdem ertönen auf dem legendären Altonaer Fischmarkt jeden Sonntag die Glocken. Ab 5 Uhr morgens – im Winter ab 7 Uhr – können Frühaufsteher nicht nur frischen Fisch, sondern auch lebende Hühner, Kaninchen und vieles andere kaufen.

🇬🇧 *In 1703, the town of Altona which is today a district of Hamburg got the right to have a market every Sunday morning before church. Since that time every Sunday ringing bells ring out over the legendary Altona Fish Market. From 5 o'clock early risers may buy not only freshly caught fish, but also living animals like chicken or rabbits and much more.*

▲ Die Fischauktionshalle wurde 1896 eröffnet. Ihre Form erinnert an eine dreischiffige Basilika.

▲ *The auction hall of the fish market was opened in 1896. It resembles a basilica with three naves.*

33

St. Pauli
St. Pauli

🇬🇧 *St. Pauli is a district of Hamburg and well known as a world of nightclubs and bars with no closing time. The red-light district is restricted to a small area around the main street called Reeperbahn, where in earlier days the rope makers had their workshops. It was here in the Star Club, that in 1962 some teenage seasonal workers from Liverpool started their careers as the "Beatles".*

🇩🇪 Der Stadtteil St. Pauli ist vor allem als Vergnügungsviertel bekannt. Letzteres beschränkt sich aber auf nur wenige Straßen rund um die Reeperbahn, wo früher die Seilmacher („Reepschläger") ihre Werkstätten hatten. In diesem behördlich festgelegten Gebiet gibt es für die Gastronomie keine Sperrstunde. Der Star-Club in St. Pauli war 1962 ein Meilenstein in der Karriere der Beatles.

► Blick auf die Welt der Nachtclubs: St. Pauli

► *View to the world of nightclubs: St. Pauli*

Freie Hansestadt Bremen
Free Hanseatic City of Bremen

▼ Blick auf Bremerhaven mit dem Alten Hafen im Vordergrund und dem Neuen Hafen.

▼ *View to Bremerhaven with the Old Port in the foreground and the New Port.*

34

Lage:	Zwei-Städte-Staat im Nordwesten Deutschlands
Fläche:	400 km²
Einwohner:	665 000
Landeshauptstadt:	Bremen
Position:	*two-city-state in the North West of Germany*
Area:	*154 sq miles*
Inhabitants:	*665,000*
Capital:	*Bremen*

▬ Die Freie Hansestadt Bremen ist das kleinste Land der Bundesrepublik Deutschland. Es wird üblicherweise zu den Stadtstaaten gerechnet, obwohl es eigentlich ein Zwei-Städte-Staat ist, der aus den Städten Bremen und Bremerhaven besteht. Bremen und Bremerhaven liegen rund 60 km auseinander. Das Gebiet dazwischen gehört zum Bundesland Niedersachsen. Die Weser, die durch Bremen fließt, mündet bei Bremerhaven in die Nordsee.

Bremen ist eine Hansestadt mit mittelalterlicher Tradition und einem heute noch bedeutenden Hafen. Durch die zunehmende Versandung der Weser wurde 1827 begonnen, einen neuen Bremer Hafen an der Wesermündung anzulegen. So entstand die Siedlung und heutige Stadt Bremerhaven.

🇬🇧 *Bremen, which was a member of the Hanseatic League, is the smallest state of the Federal Republic. It is a city-state although it actually consists of two towns: Bremen and the deep-water port Bremerhaven. The distance between both towns is about 35 miles. The country in between belongs to Lower Saxony, which is a state of the Federal Republic. The river Weser, which runs through Bremen, empties into the North Sea at Bremerhaven.*

Bremen is a city of a long medieval tradition with an important trading port. Due to the increasing silting of the river Weser, a new port was built in 1827. At the same location a settlement was established which became the town that is today named Bremerhaven.

Bremen
Bremen

Landeshauptstadt von Bremen	
Fläche:	325 km²
Einwohner:	550 000
Capital of Bremen	
Area:	*125 sq miles*
Inhabitants:	*550,000*

► Das Märchen von den Bremer Stadtmusikanten, Esel, Hund, Katze und Hahn, ist eine der bekanntesten Geschichten der Gebrüder Grimm.

► *The story of the Bremen Town Musicians, donkey, dog, cat and rooster, is one of the best known tales of the Brothers Grimm.*

◄ Das Bremer Rathaus ist als einziges Rathaus des Spätmittelalters nie zerstört worden.

◄ *The city hall of Bremen is the only one of the late Middle Ages which was never destroyed.*

▼ Rolandstatuen sind ein Symbol für städtische Rechte und Freiheit. Die Rolandstatue auf dem Bremer Marktplatz gilt als eine der schönsten.

▼ *Roland monuments are symbols of municipal rights and freedom. The Roland monument at the Bremen Marktplatz is assumed to be one of the most beautiful.*

37

■ Die Geschichte Bremens reicht bis ins 8. Jahrhundert zurück. Im Jahr 1358 trat Bremen offiziell der Hanse bei und gelangte schnell zu großer Bedeutung als Handelsstadt. Als äußeres Zeichen von Freiheit und Unabhängigkeit errichteten die Bremer Bürger 1404 die Rolandstatue und 1409 das prächtige Rathaus auf ihrem Marktplatz. Beide gehören heute zum UNESCO-Welterbe. Ebenfalls am Marktplatz liegen das Gebäude der Bremischen Bürgerschaft und die Bremer Baumwollbörse. Vom Marktplatz zur Weser führt die Böttcherstraße, die zu den Touristenattraktionen in Bremen zählt.

Sehr sehenswert ist auch der „Schnoor", der vermutlich älteste Kern von Bremen. Im 17. und 18. Jahrhundert lebten hier viele Handwerker, die Seile (Schnoor = Schnur), Ankerketten und anderes Schiffszubehör fertigten.

■ *The history of Bremen dates back to the 8th century. In 1358, Bremen became an official member of the Hanseatic League and grew quickly into a very important trading town. As a symbol of freedom and independence the citizens of Bremen installed at the Marktplatz (main square) both the statue of Roland (1404) and the great town hall (Rathaus, 1409), which are today UNESCO world heritage sites. Also at the square Marktplatz are both the state parliament building and the building of the cotton stock market. The most attractive street, Böttcherstraße, leads from here down to the river Weser.*

The so-called "Schnoor" is probably the oldest core district of Bremen. In the 17th and 18th century, many craftsmen lived there and produced ship equipment like ropes and anchor cables.

Bremerhaven
Bremerhaven

Im Jahr 1827 kaufte die Stadt Bremen dem Königreich Hannover Land an der Wesermündung ab und legte einen Hafen sowie die Siedlung Bremerhaven an. Zwanzig Jahre später wurde Bremerhaven Ausgangspunkt der ersten Dampferlinie von Europa nach Amerika. In der kurzen, aber wechselvollen Geschichte Bremerhavens wurde die Stadt mit der Nachbar- und Konkurrenzstadt Wesermünde zusammengelegt und verlor vorübergehend ihren Namen. Erst 1947 erhielt die Stadt endgültig den Namen Bremerhaven und die heutige politische Zugehörigkeit.

Der „Container-Terminal Bremerhaven" gehört zu den größten Containerhäfen der Welt und kann von den größten Schiffen tidenunabhängig erreicht werden. Eine herausragende Stellung nehmen auch die Hafenanlagen für den Automobil-Export und -Import ein. Und von der traditionellen Columbuskaje legten schon in den 1920er-Jahren die Passagierdampfer mit den europäischen Aussiedlern nach Amerika ab.

▼ Die 75,50 m lange „Seute Deern" („Süßes Mädel") ist der älteste und längste noch erhaltene Frachtensegler aus Holz. Das Schiff liegt im Museumshafen.

▼ The 250 feet long "Seute Deern" ("Sweet Girl") is the oldest and largest existing commercial sailing ship in wood. It is in the museum port of Bremerhaven.

In 1827, Bremen purchased some land from the kingdom of Hanover in order to build a new port where the river Weser joins the North Sea. Twenty years later, the new port and settlement of Bremerhaven became the starting point of the first steamer line from Europe to America. During its short history Bremerhaven was merged with Wesermünde, a competing neighbouring town, and lost its name. In 1947, the town got its name Bremerhaven back and became a member of the city-state Bremen.

The container terminal at Bremerhaven is one of the largest in the world and is independent of tidal range. The port also plays an outstanding role for car export and import. In the 1920s, passenger steamers with European emigrants left from the traditional Columbus Quay for America.

► Blick vom Weserwehr, das 1993 fertig-gestellt wurde und das alte Wehr von 1911 ersetzt. Das Weserwehr besteht aus fünf Feldern mit je 30 m Breite.

► View from the Weser weir which was built in 1993 and which replaces the old weir of 1911. The weir consists of five sectors with 150 feet in width each.

Weser
River Weser

 Die Weser ist einer der großen deut-schen Flüsse. Sie entsteht aus der Vereini-gung der Flüsse Werra und Fulda – in Hann. Münden, zwischen Kassel und Göttingen – und mündet nach 452 km bei Bremerhaven in die Nordsee. Der Oberlauf bis Bremen (Oberweser und Mittelweser) ist eine wichtige Binnenwasserstraße, die bei Minden von einer anderen Binnenwas-serstraße, dem Mittellandkanal in 13 m Höhe überquert wird. Beide Wasserstra-ßen sind durch Schleusen verbunden.

Die 85 km lange so genannte Unterweser von Bremen bis zur Nordsee ist eine See-schifffahrtsstraße, auf der andere behörd-liche Verordnungen gelten als auf Binnen-wasserstraßen.

Die Weser wird auf ihrer gesamten Länge bis zur Nordsee vom Weser-Radweg beglei-tet, einem der beliebtesten Radwanderwege in Deutschland. Er führt vom Weserberg-land durch die norddeutsche Tiefebene bis zu den Ozeanriesen in Bremerhaven.

The Weser is one of the big German rivers. It starts at the point where the rivers Werra and Fulda join, which is near the town of Hann. Mün-den, between Kassel and Göttingen. After 280 miles, the Weser joins the North Sea. The Upper Weser down to Bremen is an important inland waterway, which is crossed by a second inland waterway, the "Mittel-landkanal", at a level of 43 feet above the Weser. Both inland waterways are connected via locks.

The 55-miles section called Lower Weser from Bremen to the North Sea is a sea waterway with different traffic rules.

One of the most popular bicycle tracks in Germany leads along the river Weser from its beginning down to the North Sea. The track passes the We-serbergland (a low mountain range), then the Northern Germany Low-land and finally arrives at the ocean steamers in Bremerhaven.

Brandenburg
Brandenburg

Der Park des Schlosses Branitz, den Fürst Pückler im 19. Jahrhundert anlegte

The park of the estate Schloss Branitz founded by Prince Pückler in the 19th century

40

Lage:	im Nordosten Deutschlands
Fläche:	29 500 km²
Einwohner:	2,6 Millionen
Landeshauptstadt:	Potsdam
Position:	*in the North East of Germany*
Area:	*11,390 sq miles*
Inhabitants:	*2.6 million*
Capital:	*Potsdam*

▬ Brandenburg ist ein Bundesland, in dessen Mitte sich ein eigenständiger Stadtstaat befindet: Berlin. Brandenburg und Berlin bilden eine Metropolregion, deren Infrastruktur stark auf die Bundeshauptstadt ausgerichtet ist. Außerhalb eines gewissen Gürtels um Berlin ist das Land Brandenburg relativ dünn besiedelt.

Brandenburg gilt als das gewässerreichste Bundesland Deutschlands. Die über 3000 natürlich entstandenen Seen stammen großenteils aus der Eiszeit. Hinzu kommen unzählige künstlich angelegte Teiche und Baggerseen. Über 33 000 km Flüsse, Bäche, Kanäle und Gräben durchziehen das Land. Das bekannteste von Fließgewässern durchzogene Gebiet ist der Spreewald.

❊ *Brandenburg is a state of the Federal Republic which embraces an autonomous city-state: Berlin. Both Brandenburg and Berlin form a common central region whose infrastructure is oriented toward the capital of the Federal Republic. Outside of greater Berlin, the country of Brandenburg is thinly populated.*

No other state in Germany has more water – lakes and rivers. The more than 3,000 natural lakes are mainly relics from the last glacial epoch. They are amplified by innumerable artificial ponds and lakes. More than 20,000 miles of rivers, streams and canals run through the country. The best known region run through by water is the forest Spreewald.

Potsdam
Potsdam

Landeshauptstadt von Brandenburg	
Fläche:	187 km²
Einwohner:	150 000
Capital of Brandenburg	
Area:	*72 sq miles*
Inhabitants:	*150,000*

► Die russisch-orthodoxe Kirche Alexander Newski von 1829 ist ein Zeichen der religiösen Toleranz in Preußen.

► *The Russian Orthodox church Alexander Newski from 1829 is a symbol of religious tolerance in Prussia.*

◄ Das Holländische Viertel in der Potsdamer Altstadt wurde um 1740 für holländische Handwerker errichtet.

◄ *The Dutch Quarter of the historical city centre of Potsdam was built for Dutch craftsmen in about 1740.*

■ Potsdam ist die ehemalige Residenzstadt des Königreichs Preußen und stellt eine einzigartige Kulturlandschaft dar, die 1990 von der UNESCO in die Liste des Weltkultur- und Naturerbes der Menschheit aufgenommen wurde. Mit weitläufigen Parkanlagen und 150 Gebäuden – darunter über 20 Schlösser – ist die Berlin-Potsdamer Kulturlandschaft die größte der deutschen Welterbestätten.

Potsdams bekannteste Sehenswürdigkeit ist das Schloss Sanssouci. Sehenswert sind aber auch die historischen Bereiche der Stadt: die Russische Kolonie Alexandrowka, das Holländische Viertel und das einstige böhmische Weberviertel.

Durch seine einzigartige Lage – Parklandschaften und über 20 wassersporttaugliche Gewässer in unmittelbarer Nähe – bietet Potsdam ein umfangreiches Freizeitangebot, von dem nicht zuletzt die über 20 000 Studenten profitieren.

▨ *Potsdam is the former residence town of the Kingdom of Prussia and is a unique area of culture, which was taken into the UNESCO list of culture and nature world heritage in 1990. With widespread parks and 150 buildings – among them more than 20 palaces – the culture landscape of Berlin-Potsdam is the largest of all German world heritage sites.*

The most popular sight in Potsdam is the palace Sanssouci. However, worth seeing are also the historical districts of the town: the Russian colony Alexandrowka, the "Holländisches Viertel" (Dutch quarter) and the former Bohemian weaver quarter.

Due to its unique situation – park landscape with more than 20 lakes and rivers suited for water sports – Potsdam offers a lot of leisure activities. Last but not least more than 20,000 students enjoy them.

▼ Das „kleine" Brandenburger Tor wurde 1770 fertiggestellt und bildete den westlichen Abschluss der Altstadt.

▼ *The "small" Brandenburg Gate was built in 1770 and was the western end of the historical town.*

43

Cottbus
Cottbus

▬ Die Stadt Cottbus liegt im Südosten Brandenburgs, etwa 30 km vor der Grenze zu Polen. Cottbus ist mit rund 100 000 Einwohnern nach Potsdam die zweitgrößte Stadt des Bundeslandes. Schon im 3. Jahrhundert n. Chr. siedelten germanische Stämme im heutigen Altstadtbereich. Ab dem 6. Jahrhundert wurden sie durch slawische Stämme abgelöst und im 8. Jahrhundert siedelte hier ein westslawischer Stamm, die Lusitzi, von dem sich der heutige Name der Region, „Lausitz", ableitet. Die kulturelle Tradition dieser Zeit wird von einer kleinen Minderheit der Bevölkerung heute noch gepflegt. So wird die sorbische (wendische) Sprache noch an einigen Schulen gelehrt.

Von kulturell internationaler Bedeutung ist der Gutshof Schloss Branitz mit seiner riesigen Parkanlage, die im 19. Jahrhundert von Fürst Pückler angelegt wurde. Er nutzte den hohen Grundwasserstand der benachbarten Spree, um eine vollendete Gartenlandschaft mit Seen und Kanälen zu gestalten.

▼ Schloss Branitz steht im Zentrum einer riesigen Gartenanlage. Heute beherbergt es das Fürst-Pückler-Museum.

▼ *The palace Schloss Branitz is the centre of a large garden landscape. Today, it houses the Prince Pückler Museum.*

44

▆▆ *The town of Cottbus is located in the south-east of Brandenburg, about 20 miles from Poland. Cottbus has about 100,000 inhabitants and is – after Potsdam – the second largest town of the state. Already during the 3rd century, Germanic tribes settled in the area of the historical town. From the 6th century onward, they were replaced by Slavic tribes, who on their part were replaced in the 8th century by a further Slavic tribe, the so-called "Lusitzi", which gave the region today's name "Lausitz". The cultural tradition of that time is still cultivated by a small minority of inhabitants. Their Sorbian (Wendish) language is still being taught at some schools.*

An international highlight is the estate and palace Schloss Branitz built by Prince Pückler in the 19th century. He made use of the high ground-water level forced by the neighbouring river Spree and created a perfect garden landscape with lakes and canals around his palace.

■ Die Stadt Frankfurt an der Oder liegt im äußersten Osten Deutschlands in der brandenburgischen Auen-, Wald- und Seenlandschaft. Die Oder ist der Grenzfluss zwischen Deutschland und Polen. Sie bildet gleichzeitig die östliche Stadtgrenze.

Frankfurt (Oder) entstand im 13. Jahrhundert, als sich Kaufleute an einer Stelle der Oder ansiedelten, wo der Fluss relativ leicht zu passieren war und eine west-östliche Handelsstraße eingerichtet werden konnte. Um 1430 wurde Frankfurt Mitglied der Hanse und entwickelte sich zu einer wohlhabenden Stadt, die allerdings wegen ihrer strategischen Lage häufig in Kriege verwickelt war.

Frankfurt (Oder) war durch den „Eisernen Vorhang" Jahrzehnte lang eine Grenzstadt ohne Zugang zum Gebiet östlich der Oder. Noch gelten die Oder und das umliegende ehemalige Sumpfgebiet als Geheimtipp für Rad- und Wasserwanderer. Aber lange lässt sich das Geheimnis nicht mehr hüten.

Frankfurt on the banks of the river Oder is located in the most eastern part of Germany, the Brandenburg pastureland with wood and lakes. The river Oder marks the border to Poland. It also forms the eastern city boundary of Frankfurt.

The town was founded in the 13th century, when traders settled at a place where the river could easily be crossed and a trading route from East to West could be established. In about 1430, Frankfurt became a member of the Hanseatic League and prospered well. However, due to its strategic location, Frankfurt was frequently involved in wars.

Because of the "Iron Curtain", for some decades, Frankfurt had no access to the region east of the Oder. This is why the river Oder and its surrounding marsh area are still an insider's tip for hikers, boats and cyclists. However, the tip will probably not be kept secret any longer.

45

► Das Rathaus von Frankfurt (Oder), dessen Bau 1253 begonnen wurde, nachdem Frankfurt die Stadtrechte erhalten hatte.

► *The town hall of Frankfurt/Oder was founded in 1253 after the town had received its town charter.*

▲ Schloss Cecilienhof wurde von 1913 bis
1917 im Stil eines englischen Landhauses
erbaut. Ein Teil des Schlosses wird heute
als Hotel genutzt.

▲ *Designed in the style of an English
country manor, the palace Cecilienhof
was constructed from 1913 to 1917. A
part of the palace is used as a hotel.*

Schloss Cecilienhof
Schloss Cecilienhof

■ Schloss Cecilienhof liegt im nördlichen Teil des Neuen Gartens in Potsdam zwischen dem Heiligen See und der seeähnlich ausgeweiteten Havel. Es ist der letzte Schlossbau der Hohenzollern und wurde von Kaiser Wilhelm II. für seinen Sohn, Kronprinz Wilhelm, und dessen Gemahlin Cecilie in Auftrag gegeben. Der Gebäudekomplex entstand im englischen Landhausstil und wurde im August 1917 bezogen. Als ein Jahr später die Monarchie in Deutschland abgeschafft wurde und der Kaiser und Kronprinz ins niederländische Exil gingen, musste auch bald darauf Cecilie aus wirtschaftlichen Gründen das Schloss verlassen. 1926 konnte das Kronprinzenpaar nach Cecilienhof zurückkehren und wohnte dort bis 1945. In dieser Zeit war das Schloss ein gesellschaftlicher Mittelpunkt.

Bekannt geworden ist Cecilienhof als Tagungsort der Potsdamer Konferenz, die hier vom 17. Juli bis 2. August 1945 stattfand. Das aus vielen Gebäudeteilen mit insgesamt 176 Zimmern und fünf Innenhöfen bestehende Schloss wurde nach der Konferenz der Öffentlichkeit zugänglich gemacht und wird heute auch für Empfänge und Staatsbesuche genutzt.

🇬🇧 *The palace Schloss Cecilienhof is in the northern part of the park Neuer Garten in Potsdam, between the lake Heiliger See and the river Havel, which is expanding into a lake there. It is the most recent of all Hohenzollern dynasty buildings and was ordered by the emperor Wilhelm II as a home for his son, crown price Wilhelm, and his wife Cecilie. The buildings were designed in the style of an English country manor and were ready to be moved in by August, 1917. One year later, when the monarchy was abolished and the emperor as well as the crown prince went to the Netherlands for exile, Cecilie had to leave the palace for economic reasons. The crown prince couple could come back in 1926 and stayed there up to 1945. During this period, the palace was a central meeting point of the high society.*

Schloss Cecilienhof became well known when it served as a meeting place for the Potsdam Conference from July 17 through August 2, 1945. After the conference, the palace − many single buildings with altogether 176 rooms − was opened to the public and today is also being used for state events.

Schloss Sanssouci
Schloss Sanssouci

Das Schloss Sanssouci (frz. = „ohne Sorgen") ist heute das wohl berühmteste Schloss in Potsdam, obwohl es von seinen Erbauern keineswegs als Prunkschloss geplant war. Im Jahr 1744 ließ König Friedrich der Große von Preußen auf der Anhöhe eines kurz zuvor angelegten Weinbergs ein „kleines Weinberghäuschen" bauen. Friedrich wünschte für sich ganz allein ein ebenerdiges privates Wohnschloss, von dessen Innenräumen er direkt und ohne Stufen in den Garten gelangen konnte. Er lebte hier in den Sommermonaten ohne Gemahlin und ohne andere Frauen.

Unter König Friedrich Wilhelm IV. wurde Sanssouci etwa 100 Jahre später umgebaut und um die heutigen Seitenflügel erweitert. Friedrich der Große hatte testamentarisch verfügt, in Sanssouci neben seinen Lieblingshunden „ohne Prunk, ohne Pomp" beigesetzt zu werden. Dieser Wunsch des Königs konnte jedoch erst an seinem 205. Todestag im Jahr 1991 erfüllt werden.

The palace Schloss Sanssouci (French = "free of care") is probably the most famous palace of Potsdam, although it was by no means planned as a palace. In 1744, the Prussian King Frederick the Great ordered a "little vineyard home" to be built on the top of a recently planted vineyard. Frederick wanted a very private home at ground level from which he could enter the garden without any steps. He lived there during the summer months without his wife or any other woman.

About 100 years later, the palace was reconstructed and enhanced by side wings, as they are today. Frederick the Great wrote in his will that he should be buried "without pomp and splendour" next to his favourite dogs. The king's request could not be fulfilled until the 205th anniversary of his death in 1991.

❢ Mehr als alle anderen preußischen Königsschlösser ist Schloss Sanssouci genau auf die Persönlichkeit von König Friedrich dem Großen zugeschnitten.

❢ *More than all other royal Prussian palaces, the palace Schloss Sanssouci is strictly tailored to the personality of King Frederick the Great.*

47

Spree und Spreewald
River Spree and the Spreewald

■ Der Spreewald ist eine Auen- und Moor-landschaft im Südosten Brandenburgs, die vor nicht mehr als 20 000 Jahren entstand. Damals behinderten Gletscher den Lauf der Spree, sodass diese sich ausbreitete und zu sehr vielen kleinen Flussläufen verzweigte. Alle Flussläufe ergeben zusammen mit den künstlich angelegten Kanälen eine Gesamt-länge von 970 km. Im Jahr 1991 erhielt der Spreewald die Anerkennung der UNESCO als Biosphärenreservat.

Durch den Spreewald führen relativ wenige Straßen. Weite Gebiete und manche landwirt-schaftlichen Anwesen sind nur auf dem Was-serweg zu erreichen. Im Spreewald verkehren ausschließlich „handgestakte" Kähne, die mit-tels langer Stangen von Hand angetrieben wer-den. Motorboote gibt es hier nicht. Die Kahn-fahrten im Spreewald sind eine herausragende Attraktion des Tourismus in Brandenburg.

Die eingelegten Spreewälder Gurken sind eine bekannte kulinarische Spezialität der Region.

⊞ *The Spreewald is a marshy region in the south-east of Brandenburg which was formed about 20,000 years ago. At that time, glaciers obstructed the course of the river Spree and caused the river to expand and to create many small rivers and canals. Altogether, including some artificial canals, they add up to a total length of 600 miles. In 1991, the Spreewald was designated as one of the UNESCO World Biosphere Reserves.*

Very few roads lead through the Spreewald. Large areas as well as some agricultural estates can be accessed only on waterways. Within the Spreewald, there are only punts, which are moved by one person using a long stick. Motor boats are not in use. The Spreewald boat trips are an extraordinary attraction for tourists in Brandenburg.

A well-known local Spreewald speciality are the pickled gherkins.

▼ 200 traditionelle Kahnfährleute füh-ren die Touristen durch den Spreewald.

▼ *200 traditional ferrymen take tourists through the Spreewald region.*

Havel
River Havel

▬ Die Havel ist ein erstaunlicher Fluss. Sie entspringt in Mecklenburg-Vorpommern, durchfließt Brandenburg und Berlin und mündet in Sachsen-Anhalt in die Elbe. Sie hat zwar eine Länge von 325 km. Aber die Mündung ist nur 70 km von der Quelle entfernt. Im Großraum Berlin und Potsdam bildet die langsam fließende Havel viele, teilweise relativ große Seen, die zusammen ein äußerst beliebtes Wassersportrevier ergeben.

🇬🇧 *The river Havel is quite astonishing. Its origin is in Mecklenburg-Lower Pomerania, it runs through Brandenburg and Berlin and finally joins the river Elbe in Saxony-Anhalt. The total length of the river is 200 miles, but the distance from the source to the mouth is only 43 miles. Within the greater area of Berlin and Potsdam the slowly flowing river expands into many lakes, some of which are relatively large and very popular water sports areas.*

◄ Werder mit der Havel im Vordergrund

◄ *The town of Werder with the river Havel in the foreground*

49

Uckermark
Uckermark

▬ Die Uckermark ist eine Region im äußersten Nordosten des Landes Brandenburg an der Grenze zu Polen. Die Einwohnerentwicklung ist zwar – wirtschaftlich bedingt – tendenziell rückläufig. Touristisch ist jedoch ein Aufschwung zu verzeichnen, der den drei großen Schutzgebieten Nationalpark Unteres Odertal, Biosphärenreservat Schorfheide-Chorin und Naturpark Uckermärkische Seen zu verdanken ist.

🇬🇧 *The Uckermark is a region in the very north east of Brandenburg next to Poland. For economical reasons, the number of inhabitants is tending to decrease. However thanks to tourists, an upturn is being experienced. Three large protected areas make the region attractive: the national park Unteres Odertal, the Biosphere Reserves Schorfheide-Chorin and the natural park Uckermärkische Seen.*

► Die kleine romantische Holzkirche im Dorf Seehausen wird häufig für Hochzeiten genutzt.

► *The small romantic wooden church in the village of Seehausen is frequently used for weddings.*

Niedersachsen
Lower Saxony

Das „Grundlose Moor" ist eines der wenigen noch vollkommen intakten Moore Niedersachsens.

The "Grundlose Moor" is one of the few absolutely virgin moors in Lower Saxony.

Lage:	Nordwestdeutschland
Fläche:	47 600 km²
Einwohner:	8 Millionen
Landeshauptstadt:	Hannover
Position:	*in the North West of Germany*
Area:	*18,380 sq miles*
Inhabitants:	*8 million*
Capital:	*Hanover*

■ Der Name „Niedersachsen" geht auf den germanischen Volksstamm der Sachsen zurück, die sich während der Völkerwanderungszeit ab dem 3. Jahrhundert hier niederließen und ausbreiteten.

Niedersachsen ist der Fläche nach das zweitgrößte Land der Bundesrepublik und eines der landschaftlich vielfältigsten: Im Nordwesten die Nordseeküste, im Südosten der Harz als Mittelgebirge und in der Mitte fruchtbare landwirtschaftliche Gebiete oder auch Heidelandschaften wie die Lüneburger Heide.

Entsprechend vielfältig sind auch die touristischen Angebote des Landes. Zentren des Fremdenverkehrs sind insbesondere die Seebäder an der Nordseeküste – Cuxhaven und Umgebung – sowie die Ostfriesischen Inseln.

⬛ *The name Lower Saxony is derived from the Germanic tribe which settled in this area since the migration of people from the 3rd century onward.*

In terms of square miles, Lower Saxony is the second largest state of the Federal Republic. And it is of great scenic variety: the coast of the North Sea in the north-west, the low mountain Harz area in the south-east, and in the middle of the state the fertile agricultural areas or areas of heath land like the Lüneburger Heide.

The offers for tourists show a similar variety. Tourist centres are especially the sea resorts at the North Sea, for instance the Cuxhaven region as well as the East Frisian Islands.

Hannover
Hanover

Landeshauptstadt von Schleswig-Holstein	
Fläche:	200 km²
Einwohner:	516 000
Capital of Schleswig-Holstein	
Area:	*77 sq miles*
Inhabitants:	*516,000*

► Der Maschteich mit dem Rathaus von Hannover, das 1913 gebaut wurde und auf Buchenpfählen steht

► *The small lake Maschteich with the city hall of Hanover from 1913 which was built on beechwood stilts*

◄ Die Königlichen Gärten Herrenhausen wurden vor 300 Jahren angelegt.

◄ The royal gardens Herrenhausen were planted 300 years ago.

▬ Hannover entstand aus einer mittelalterlichen Siedlung am Ufer der Leine. Im 17. Jahrhundert wurde Hannover Residenzstadt und 1714 wurde Kurfürst Georg Ludwig als Georg I. gleichzeitig König von England. Bis 1837 wurden die Königreiche Großbritannien und Hannover in Personalunion regiert. Zwischen beiden Adelshäusern bestehen heute noch enge Beziehungen.

Das heutige Hannover ist eine moderne Industriestadt und ein zentraler Verkehrsknotenpunkt. Und nicht zuletzt ist Hannover als Messestadt weltbekannt.

Zu den herausragenden Sehenswürdigkeiten in Hannover gehören die Herrenhäuser Gärten, die sich aus dem Großen Garten, dem Berggarten sowie dem Georgen- und Welfengarten zusammensetzen. Der Große Garten zählt zu den bedeutendsten Barockgärten Europas und wird in den Sommermonaten unter anderem für Musik- und Theaterveranstaltungen genutzt.

⬛ *The city of Hanover emerged from a medieval settlement at the bank of the river Leine. In the 17th century, Hanover became a residence town, and in 1714, the electoral prince Georg Ludwig also became king of England as George 1st. Up to 1837, Hanover and England shared the same ruler. Both aristocratic families are well connected still today.*

Hanover is now a modern industrial city and a central traffic junction. Of international reputation are the annual trade fairs.

Among the exceptional sights of Hanover are the four gardens Herrenhäuser Gärten. One of these gardens, the Großer Garten, is one of the most important Baroque gardens in Europe. During the summer months, the garden is used for music events and theatre festivals.

► Das Bomann-Museum in Celle ist eines der bedeutendsten Museen in Niedersachsen.

► The Bomann Museum in Celle is one of the most significant museums in Lower Saxony.

Celle
Celle

▬ Die Stadt Celle liegt etwa 30 km nordöstlich von Hannover. Vom 15. bis zum 17. Jahrhundert erlebte Celle eine wirtschaftliche Blüte, die sich in vielen heute noch erhaltenen Bauwerken niederschlug. So ist die Altstadt insgesamt eine Hauptattraktion der Stadt. Etwa 480 Fachwerkhäuser sind hier entweder in ihrem Originalzustand erhalten oder restauriert worden.

Das Celler Schloss war ursprünglich eine mittelalterliche Wasserburg, die in der Renaissance weitgehend ihre heutige Gestalt bekam. Im Schloss befindet sich das noch bespielte Schlosstheater aus dem Jahre 1671.

⬛ *The town of Celle is about 20 miles north-east of Hanover. From the 15th through the 17th century, the town prospered as can be seen from many buildings which are preserved up to now. The old town centre as a whole is the main attraction of the city. About 480 half-timbered houses are either in their original condition or are restored.*

The medieval castle of Celle was originally a moated castle and got its current shape mainly during the time of Renaissance. The theatre of the castle was built in 1671 and is still in operation.

Göttingen
Göttingen

▬ Die Stadt Göttingen liegt im äußersten Süden von Niedersachsen inmitten einer waldreichen Hügellandschaft. Göttingen ist vor allem durch seine 1737 gegründete Universität berühmt. Die Brüder Jacob und Wilhelm Grimm, die Märchensammler, waren hier Professoren, ebenso der Mathematiker Carl Friedrich Gauß und nicht zuletzt forschten eine ganze Reihe von Nobelpreisträgern in Göttingen, darunter Max Born und Werner Heisenberg.

🇬🇧 *The town of Göttingen is in the very south of Lower Saxony and is surrounded by wooded hills. Göttingen is famous for its university which was founded in 1737. Teachers at the university were among others the famous collectors of fairy tales Jacob and Wilhelm Grimm, the mathematician Carl Friedrich Gauß, and a number of Nobel prize-winners like Max Born and Werner Heisenberg researched in Göttingen.*

▲ Das Aulagebäude am Wilhelmsplatz, Sitz des Präsidiums und zentraler Veranstaltungsort der Georg-August-Universität in Göttingen

▲ *The assembly hall next to the Wilhelmsplatz, domicile of the Presidential Board and central venue of the Georg-August-University in Göttingen*

Hameln
Hamelin

▬ Nordwestlich von Göttingen liegt im Weserbergland die Stadt Hameln. Die Weser fließt durch die Stadt, an deren Ort bereits eine steinzeitliche Siedlung nachgewiesen ist. Weltweite Bekanntheit erlangte die Stadt durch die Sage vom Rattenfänger von Hameln, die sich aus einer Überlieferung aus dem Jahre 1284 entwickelte. Noch heute nennt sich die Stadt offiziell „Rattenfängerstadt Hameln".

🇬🇧 *North-west of Göttingen, located in the low mountain area Weserbergland, is the town of Hamelin. The river Weser runs through the town, where settlements from the Stone Age have been found. The town became famous by the legend of the rat-catcher, which was derived from records of the year 1284. Still today, the town is officially named town of the Pied Piper of Hamelin.*

◄ Der Rattenfänger ist das Wahrzeichen der Stadt Hameln.

◄ *The Pied Piper is the symbol of the town of Hamelin.*

Osnabrück
Osnabrück

🇩🇪 Die Stadt Osnabrück ist mit 163 000 Einwohnern die drittgrößte Stadt in Niedersachsen. Sie liegt im Westen an der Grenze zu Nordrhein-Westfalen. Die Entwicklung zur Stadt wurde eingeleitet, als Karl der Große im Jahr 780 hier einen Bischofssitz gründete. Osnabrück nennt sich „Friedensstadt", weil unter anderem hier der Westfälische Friede, der den Dreißigjährigen Krieg beendete, ausgehandelt wurde.

🇬🇧 *The city of Osnabrück has 163,000 inhabitants and is the third largest city in Lower Saxony. Its location is in the west, close to North Rhine-Westphalia. The development of the town started in 780 when Charlemagne founded a bishop's see. Osnabrück calls itself "town of peace". The Peace of Westphalia, which ended the Thirty Years' War, was signed here and announced from the town hall steps.*

▲ Das Rathaus des Westfälischen Friedens in Osnabrück

▲ *The town hall of Osnabrück where the Peace of Westphalia was signed*

Oldenburg
Oldenburg

🇩🇪 Etwa 45 km westlich von Bremen, an der alten Handelsstraße nach Jever, wurde zu Beginn des 12. Jahrhunderts eine „Zollstation" errichtet, die später zur Stadt Oldenburg heranwuchs. Nach einer wechselvollen Geschichte hat Oldenburg heute rund 160 000 Einwohner. Die Stadt besitzt einen wirtschaftlich bedeutsamen Hafen, der für Binnenschiffe und für kleinere Seeschiffe über die Weser erreichbar ist.

🇬🇧 *It was the beginning of the 12th century, when about 30 miles west of Bremen a customs house was built on an old trading route to the town of Jever. This is the origin of the town of Oldenburg. After a varied history Oldenburg has today about 160,000 inhabitants. The port of Oldenburg is important and can be accessed both by inland ships and – via the river Weser – by small sea-going ships.*

◄ Dieser Pulverturm diente zur Lagerung von Schwarzpulver und war Teil der Stadtmauer.

◄ *This so-called powder tower was used as a storeroom for black powder and was part of the historical town wall.*

Lüneburg
Lüneburg

🇩🇪 Lüneburg liegt am nördlichen Rand der nach ihr benannten Lüneburger Heide und etwa 50 km südöstlich von Hamburg. Die frühesten Spuren menschlicher Anwesenheit sind etwa 150 000 Jahre alt. Die Lüneburger Altstadt liegt über einem Salzstock, dem die Stadt die Monopolstellung als Salzlieferant zum Pökeln der Nordsee- und Ostseeheringe und die frühe Mitgliedschaft in der Hanse zu verdanken hatte. Mit dem Niedergang der Hanse im späten 16. Jahrhundert kam die Bautätigkeit in Lüneburg zum Erliegen, sodass das historische Stadtbild weitgehend erhalten blieb.

🇬🇧 *The town of Lüneburg is about 30 miles south-east of Hamburg at the northern edge of the heath land Lüneburger Heide. The oldest traces from human beings are about 150,000 years old. The old town centre is located over a salt mine, which gave the town a monopoly on salt deliveries to the North Sea and Baltic fish traders. This is why Lüneburg became an early member of the Hanseatic League. When in the late 16th century the Hanseatic League declined, the development of the town came to a standstill. As a consequence, the historical townscape is largely preserved.*

56

▲ Gartenfest vor Schloss Clemenswerth

▲ *Summer festival at Schloss Clemenswerth*

Emsland
Emsland

🇩🇪 Das Land, durch das die Ems fließt – das ist das Emsland. Im Westen grenzt es an die Niederlande, im Süden reicht es bis nach Nordrhein-Westfalen. Die größte Stadt des Emslandes ist Lingen mit ihrem gut erhaltenen historischen Marktplatz, auf dem alle drei Jahre zu Pfingsten das Kivelingsfest, ein mittelalterliches Spektakel, stattfindet. Jedes Jahr am letzten Samstag im August findet in Sögel rund um das Schloss Clemenswerth ein großes Gartenfest mit vielen Künstlern statt. Bekannt ist das Emsland durch die weltweit einzige Versuchsanlage für die Transrapid-Magentschwebebahn und die Meyer Werft in Papenburg, wo Kreuzfahrtschiffe gebaut werden.

🇬🇧 *The country through which the river Ems runs – this is Emsland. In the west, it is next to the Netherlands. To the south, it extends into North Rhine-Westphalia. The biggest town of Emsland is Lingen with its well preserved historical centre where the Kivelings festival, a great medieval festival, takes place every third year at Whitsun. Every year on the last Saturday of August a great summer festival with a lot of artists takes place in Sögel around Schloss Clemenswerth. Emsland is known by its experimental installation of the Transrapid magnetic levitation railway and the Meyer Werft in Papenburg where cruise liners are built.*

Lüneburger Heide
Lüneburger Heide

🟦 Die Lüneburger Heide ist eine große Heide- und Wald-
landschaft im Nordosten Niedersachsens. Den Kern bilden
drei Naturparks, von denen der größte eine Fläche von
1130 km² hat. Um zu verhindern, dass die Heide durch
Bäume zuwächst, lässt man regelmäßig Schafe, die einheimischen Heidschnucken, die Flächen abweiden. Sie gehören ebenso wie der Wacholder zum typischen Bild der
Lüneburger Heide.

🇬🇧 *The Lüneburger Heide is a large area of heath land and*
forest in the north east of Lower Saxony. The core area is
three natural parks, the largest of which is about 440 sq
miles. The local breed of sheep, called Heidschnucken, is
kept here in order to prevent the heath land from being cov-
ered with woods. The sheep as well as the juniper trees are
typical of the Lüneburger Heide.

◄ Von Juli bis Mitte September sorgen verschiedene blühende
Heidearten für eine bunte Lüneburger Heide.

◄ *From July to mid-September, different kinds of blooming heather*
make a colourful landscape of the Lüneburger Heide.

Harz
Harz

🟦 Der Harz ist das nördlichste Mittelgebirge Deutschlands mit
dem 1141 m hohen Brocken als höchstem Berg. Der Brocken gilt
in der Literatur – auch in Goethes „Faust" – seit dem späten Mittelalter als „Hexentreffpunkt". Zusammen mit Sachsen-Anhalt
hat Niedersachsen im Jahr 2006 den Nationalpark Harz gebildet.
Der Fremdenverkehr ist für die Kurorte im Harz sowohl im Som-
mer als auch im Winter ein bedeutender Wirtschaftsfaktor.

🇬🇧 *The Harz is the most northern low mountain range of Ger-*
many. Its highest peak is the 3,743-feet Brocken. From the Middle
Ages onward, the literature – even Goethe's "Faust" – describes
the Brocken as "the meeting point of witches". Lower Saxony and
Saxony-Anhalt in cooperation established the national park Harz
in 2006. Tourism is a major economic factor for the Harz spas in
summertime as well as in wintertime.

► Die Felsen im Harz sind ein ideales Klettergebiet, nicht zuletzt
auch für Anfänger.

► *The rocky Harz is an ideal region for climbers, also for beginners.*

Ostfriesische Inseln
East Frisian Islands

Die Ostfriesischen Inseln liegen wie eine Barriere vor der deutschen und niederländischen Nordseeküste. Sieben Inseln sind bewohnt. Von Westen nach Osten sind dies Borkum, Juist, Norderney, Baltrum, Langeoog, Spiekeroog und Wangerooge. Die im Wesentlichen aus Dünen bestehenden Inseln bieten zum offenen Meer hin breite Sandstrände. Einige der Inseln sind bei Ebbe vom Festland aus per Wattwanderung zu erreichen.

Auf Borkum, der mit 32 km² Fläche größten und zugleich westlichsten Insel, leben etwa 5500 Menschen. Borkum ist seit 1830 Badeort. Vom Fährhafen zum Ortskern führt eine 7,5 km lange Inselbahnstrecke, auf der eine historische Dampflok verkehrt. Ansonsten ist das Fahrrad das wichtigste Verkehrsmittel auf Borkum.

The East Frisian Islands lie as a belt in front of the German and Dutch coast of the North Sea. Seven islands are populated. These are – from West to East – Borkum, Juist, Norderney, Baltrum, Langeoog, Spiekeroog and Wangerooge. The islands which are mainly sand dunes have wide sandy beaches. At low tide, some of the islands can be reached from the mainland by hiking through the mud flats.

The 12 sq mile island Borkum is the largest and also the most western of these islands. About 5,500 people live in Borkum, which has been a sea resort since 1830. A five mile long railway with a historic steam engine leads from the ferry port to the town centre. Besides of that, the bicycle is the vehicle type number one.

► Bis 1988 diente das Feuerschiff „Borkumriff" als Leuchtfeuer für Schiffe aus aller Welt.

► *Until 1988, the lightship "Borkumriff" was used to guide ships from all over the world.*

▼ Der endlose Sandstrand und die Nordstrand-Promenade auf Borkum

▼ *The endless sandy beach and the northern beach promenade of Borkum Island*

Cuxhaven
Cuxhaven

🇩🇪 Cuxhaven, eine Stadt mit 52 000 Einwohnern, liegt direkt an der Mündung der Elbe in die Nordsee und ist nach Bremerhaven der wichtigste deutsche Fischereihafen. Seit 1964 ist Cuxhaven aber auch staatlich anerkanntes Seeheilbad mit jährlich über 3 Millionen Übernachtungen – mehr als jeder andere Kurort in Deutschland. Das Wahrzeichen der Stadt ist die Kugelbake, ein hölzernes Seezeichen an der Elbemündung.

🇬🇧 *The town of Cuxhaven with 52,000 inhabitants is situated on the shore of the North Sea at the mouth of the river Elbe. It is – after Bremerhaven – the most important fishing port. In 1964, Cuxhaven became an official sea resort with now more than three million overnight stays per year. The symbol of the town is the "Kugelbake", a wooden marker buoy at the mouth of the river Elbe.*

► Seit 1703 ist die 30 m hohe Kugelbake das Wahrzeichen von Cuxhaven.

► *Since 1703, the 90 feet wooden marker buoy has been the symbol of Cuxhaven.*

Berlin
Berlin

▼ Der Berliner Fernsehturm am Alexanderplatz. Rechts im Vordergrund das Rote
Rathaus.

▼ *The Berlin TV tower at the square
Alexanderplatz. On the right side in the
foreground is the so-called Red Townhall.*

60

Lage:	Stadtstaat, umgeben vom Bundesland Brandenburg
Fläche:	892 km²
Einwohner:	3,4 Millionen
Position:	*city-state surrounded by the state of Brandenburg*
Area:	*344 sq miles*
Inhabitants:	*3.4 million*

■■ Berlin ist Bundeshauptstadt und Regierungssitz der Bundesrepublik Deutschland. Der Stadtstaat ist vom Bundesland Brandenburg umgeben. Berlin ist der Einwohnerzahl nach hinter London die zweitgrößte Stadt der Europäischen Union. Die größte Ausdehnung der Stadt – in Ost-West-Richtung – beträgt etwa 45 km.

Der Westen Berlins wird von der Havel, die stellenweise einer Seenlandschaft ähnelt, durchflossen. Im westlichsten der zwölf Bezirke, in Spandau, mündet die Spree in die Havel. Der Name Berlin taucht urkundlich erstmals im Jahre 1244 auf. Erst 1648 nach dem Ende des Dreißigjährigen Krieges wuchs die Stadt von damals 6000 Bürgern auf eine Million Einwohner etwa im Jahr 1875.

■■ *Berlin is the capital of the Federal Republic and location of the Federal Government. The city-state is surrounded by the state of Brandenburg. In terms of inhabitants, Berlin is the second largest city of the European Union – after London. The extension of the city is – from east to west – 28 miles.*

The river Havel, which in some places looks like a lake, runs through the western part of Berlin. In Spandau, which is the most western of the twelve Berlin districts, the river Spree joins the river Havel. The name "Berlin" was recorded in 1244 for the first time. It was not before the end of the Thirty Years' War (1648) that Berlin grew from 6,000 inhabitants to one million in 1875.

Berlin
Berlin

► Der neue Amtssitz
des Bundeskanzlers

► *The new official residence of the Chancellor
of the Federal Republic*

◄ Das Brandenburger Tor ist das wichtigste Wahrzeichen Berlins. Es wird gekrönt durch eine geflügelte Siegesgöttin, die einen von vier Pferden gezogenen Wagen (Quadriga) in die Stadt hineinlenkt.

◄ The Brandenburger Tor is the most significant symbol of Berlin. On the top is the goddess of victory driving on a horse car into the city.

▬ Vom 15. Jahrhundert bis zum Ende des ersten Weltkriegs regierte das Haus Hohenzollern in Berlin: als Markgrafen von Brandenburg, als Könige von Preußen und als deutsche Kaiser. Der Status als Residenzstadt der Könige und Hauptstadt des Deutschen Reichs hat das Stadtbild Berlins nachhaltig geprägt.

Berlin gehört zu den beliebtesten Reisezielen. Die Stadt verfügt über das größte Kongresszentrum Europas, über das größte Kaufhaus des europäischen Kontinents und über unzählige kulturelle Sehenswürdigkeiten.

Auch die Angebote für Naturfreunde und Wassersportler sind beachtenswert. Berlin besitzt die größte Stadtwaldfläche Deutschlands, darunter den Grunewald. Unter den zahlreichen Seen ist der von der Havel durchflossene Große Wannsee nicht der größte, aber sicherlich der bekannteste.

🇬🇧 *From the 15th century up to end of World War I, the Hohenzollern family ruled in Berlin: as margraves of Brandenburg, as kings of Prussia and as German emperors. The role as a royal residence town and capital has had a lasting influence on the face of Berlin.*

The city belongs to the most favourite destinations at all. Berlin has the largest congress centre in Europe, the biggest department store on the European continent and countless cultural sights.

Also the offers for nature-lovers and water sportsmen are remarkable. Berlin has the largest town forest in Germany with the Grunewald as a part of it. Among the numerous lakes, the Große Wannsee, an expansion of the river Havel, is not the largest, but certainly the best known one.

▼ Das historische Reichstagsgebäude (rechts im Bild) ist seit 1999 Sitz des Deutschen Bundestages. Im Hintergrund Neubauten der Bundesregierung.

▼ Since 1999, the historical building Reichstagsgebäude (on the right side) is the seat of the parliament of the Federal Republic.

63

Schloss Charlottenburg
Schloss Charlottenburg

Das Schloss Charlottenburg im Bezirk Charlottenburg-Wilmersdorf wurde 1695 bis 1699 als „einfaches" Sommerhaus erbaut. Nur zwei Jahre später erweiterte der neu gekrönte König Friedrich I. in Preußen das Schloss zu einer prachtvollen Anlage und nannte es 1705 seiner verstorbenen Gemahlin Charlotte zu Ehren Charlottenburg. Das legendäre Bernsteinzimmer war ursprünglich als Ausstattung für das Schloss Charlottenburg geplant, wurde jedoch 1716 dem russischen Zaren Peter dem Großen zum Geschenk gemacht.

The palace Schloss Charlottenburg, located in the Berlin district Charlottenburg-Wilmersdorf, has been built from 1695 through 1699 as a "simple" summer home. Only two years later, the recently crowned Prussian King Frederick I extended the building and built a great palace, which he named after his wife Charlotte, who had died in 1705. The legendary Amber Room was originally planned for Schloss Charlottenburg. In 1716 however, it was given to the Russian tsar Peter the Great as a present.

Schloss Charlottenburg. Im Vordergrund das Tor zum Ehrenhof.

Charlottenburg palace. In the foreground is the gate to the so-called court of honour.

Schloss Bellevue
Schloss Bellevue

▬ Das Schloss Bellevue ist seit 1994 der erste Amtssitz des deutschen Bundespräsidenten. Dem Bundespräsidenten Roman Herzog diente es bis 1998 gleichzeitig als Wohnung. Das Schloss liegt am Spreeufer in der Nähe des Reichstagsgebäudes. Den Namen Bellevue (frz. „schöne Aussicht") erhielt das 1786 von Ferdinand von Preußen errichtete Schloss wegen des schönen Ausblicks auf die Spree.

🇬🇧 *Since 1994, the palace Schloss Bellevue has been the prime residence of the President of the Federal Republic. President Roman Herzog also used the palace as his private home until 1998. The palace was built in 1786 by Ferdinand of Prussia and is located at the banks of the river Spree not far from the German Parliament. The name Bellevue (French = "beautiful view") was given because of the lovely view down to the river Spree.*

◄ Das Schloss Bellevue dient als Amtssitz des Bundespräsidenten.

◄ *The palace Bellevue is today the official residence of the President of the Federal Republic.*

Gedächtniskirche
Gedächtniskirche

▬ Die Kaiser-Wilhelm-Gedächtniskirche auf dem Breitscheidplatz am Kurfürstendamm hatte vor ihrer Zerstörung im Jahr 1943 den mit 113 m höchsten Turm der Stadt. Die 68 m hohe Turmruine blieb nach dem Krieg als Mahnmal stehen. An ihrer Seite wurde ein Kirchenneubau errichtet und 1961 eingeweiht. Inzwischen gilt die Gedächtniskirche als wichtiges Denkmal der Nachkriegsmoderne und als eines der Wahrzeichen Berlins.

🇬🇧 *The Kaiser-Wilhelm-Memorial-Church is at the boulevard Kurfürstendamm. Before it was damaged in 1943, the 370-feet church tower was the highest of the city. The tower ruin with a height of 223 feet was kept after the war as a memorial. The new octagonal church Kaiser-Wilhelm-Memorial-Church is an important symbol of post-war architecture and one of the symbols of Berlin.*

► Die Gedächtniskirche mit der Turmruine der alten Kirche im Hintergrund

► *The church Kaiser-Wilhelm-Memorial-Church with the old tower ruin in the background*

Siegessäule
Triumphal Column

▬ Die Siegessäule steht im Großen Tiergarten, einer riesigen Parkanlage in der Nähe des Regierungsviertels. Sie wurde 1873 als Nationaldenkmal der so genannten Einigungskriege erbaut. Im Inneren der Säule führt eine Wendeltreppe mit 285 Stufen zu einer 50 m hoch gelegenen Aussichtsplattform. Von dort aus hat man einen sehr schönen Überblick über das umliegende Stadtgebiet, den Potsdamer Platz und das Brandenburger Tor.

🇬🇧 *The triumphal column is in the Großer Tiergarten, which is a large park not far from the government district. The column was built in 1873 as national memorial of the Prussian-Danish war of 1864. Within the column, a spiral staircase of 285 steps leads 164 feet up to an observation deck, which offers a fine view over the surrounding city, the Potsdamer Platz and the Brandenburger Tor.*

► Die Siegesgöttin Viktoria wird von den Berlinern „Goldelse" genannt.

► *The goddess of victory, Victoria, on the top of the Triumphal Column.*

Funkturm
Radio Tower Berlin

▬ Der Berliner Funkturm ist ein alter Sendeturm auf dem Areal des Berliner Messegeländes. Er wurde anlässlich der Dritten Großen Deutschen Funkausstellung 1926 eröffnet und steht heute als eines der Wahrzeichen der Stadt unter Denkmalschutz. In 125 m Höhe befindet sich eine Aussichtsplattform. Am 22. März 1935 wurde von seiner Spitze aus das erste reguläre Fernsehprogramm der Welt abgestrahlt.

🇬🇧 *The Radio Tower Berlin (Berliner Funkturm) is a historic transmitting tower on the grounds of the exhibition centre. It was put into operation during the third German Radio Exhibition in 1926 and is today a protected symbol of Berlin. At the height of 410 feet there is an observation deck. On March 22, 1935, the first regular television program of the world was transmitted from the top of the tower.*

◄ Der 600 Tonnen schwere Funkturm steht auf elektrisch isolierten „Porzellanfüßen".

◄ *With a weight of 600,000 kilograms, the Radio Tower is electrically isolated on feet made from porcelain.*

Berliner Dom
Berlin Cathedral

Der Berliner Dom entspringt dem Wunsch des preußischen Königs und Deutschen Kaisers Wilhelm II., ein repräsentatives Gotteshaus in der Reichshauptstadt zu errichten. So wurde der Abriss des alten Doms auf der Berliner Spreeinsel und an derselben Stelle der Neubau eines Doms im Stile der italienischen Hochrenaissance in Auftrag gegeben. Nach elfjähriger Bauzeit wurde der Dom 1905 eingeweiht. In nächster Nähe befand sich das in DDR-Zeiten abgerissene Stadtschloss.

Der im Krieg stark beschädigte Dom wurde bis zum Jahr 2002 restauriert, wobei allerdings viele gestalterische Elemente vereinfacht wurden.

Die Vorgängerkirche wurde bereits 1536 zum Dom geweiht. Seit dieser Zeit finden hier die Hohenzollern ihre letzte Ruhestätte. Die Hohenzollerngruft – unter anderem mit den Prunksarkophagen des ersten Preußenkönigs Friedrich I. und seiner Gemahlin Sophie Charlotte – befindet sich unter der Kirche.

The Berlin Cathedral results from the desire of the Prussian king and German Emperor Wilhelm II to have a representative church in his capital. So the old cathedral on the Berlin Spree Island was pulled down and the new Renaissance style church was built at the same place. After eleven years of construction, the cathedral was consecrated in 1905. Next to the cathedral was the royal city palace which was pulled down after World War II.

The severely damaged cathedral was restored by 2002, however to a greater part in a simplified form.

The predecessor church was consecrated already in 1536. Since that time the church has served as the final resting place of the Hohenzollern family. The Hohenzollern Crypt with – besides others – the magnificent sarcophagi of the first Prussian King Frederick I and his wife Sophie Charlotte is located beneath the dome.

▼ Blick auf das Hauptportal des Doms. Die Parkanlage davor ist der Lustgarten.

▼ *View to the main entrance of the cathedral with the park area called Lustgarten in front of it.*

▬ Der Kurfürstendamm wurde um 1542 für die Kurfürsten als Reitweg vom Berliner Stadtschloss (in der Stadtmitte beim Dom) zum Jagdschloss Grunewald (im Südwesten der Stadt) angelegt. Der Name „Churfürsten Damm" tauchte erstmals im späten 18. Jahrhundert auf. Im Jahr 1875 veranlasste Otto von Bismarck, dass die Straße auf 53 m Breite und zu einer Prachtstraße ausgebaut wurde.

Anfang des 20. Jahrhunderts entwickelte sich der Kurfürstendamm („Ku'damm") zu einem kulturellen Zentrum und wurde zu einem Inbegriff der „Goldenen Zwanziger Jahre". Durch die Teilung Berlins nach dem zweiten Weltkrieg und mit dem Wiederaufbau entwickelte sich hier das Geschäftszentrum West-Berlins.

Mit dem Fall der Berliner Mauer verlagerte sich der Schwerpunkt vieler Investitionen in den Bezirk Berlin-Mitte und in das neue Viertel am Potsdamer Platz. Der Kurfürstendamm entwickelt sich heute mehr zu einer exklusiven Einkaufsstraße.

🏴󠁧󠁢󠁥󠁮󠁧󠁿 *The boulevard Kurfürstendamm was created in 1542 as a path for horsemen leading from the city palace (next to the cathedral) to the hunting lodge Grunewald in the south-west of Berlin. Its name came up in the late 18th century. In 1875, Otto von Bismarck ordered that the road had to be expanded into a splendid 175-feet-wide boulevard.*

During the early 20th century, the Kurfürstendamm ("Ku'damm") became a cultural centre and was the personification of the "Golden Twenties". After World War II the boulevard developed into the business centre of Western Berlin.

After the German reunification, the focus of many investment projects was relocated to the former Eastern Berlin district Berlin-Mitte and the completely newly created area at the historical traffic junction Potsdamer Platz. The boulevard Kurfürstendamm is now developing into a top shopping mile.

❮ Das neue „Kranzler-Eck" vereint das alte Café Kranzler mit moderner Büro-Architektur.

❮ *The new "Kranzler-Eck" joins the historical cafe Kranzler with modern office architecture.*

68

Potsdamer Platz
Potsdamer Platz

▬ Der Potsdamer Platz, einst einer der belebtesten Plätze Europas und während der Teilung Berlins ein öder, unbesiedelter Grenzstreifen, war nach 1990 die größte Baustelle Europas und hat sich zu einem komplett neuen Viertel entwickelt. Die führenden Architekten der Welt errichteten hier Firmenhochhäuser, Luxushotels und die „Potsdamer Platz Arkaden", eine Art überdachte Einkaufsstraße.

⚏ *The square Potsdamer Platz once was one of the busiest squares in Europe. However, as long as Berlin was divided, it was a waste and unpopulated border zone. After 1990, the Potsdamer Platz area became the largest construction site in Europe and is now a completely new city area. Leading architects of the world created high-rise buildings, luxury hotels and the "Potsdamer Platz Arcades", a covered shopping street.*

◄ Das Sony Center am Potsdamer Platz ist eine moderne Lebenswelt, die Geschäft und Unterhaltung vereint.

◄ *The Sony Center at the square Potsdamer Platz is a modern world of living with business and entertainment.*

Unter den Linden
Unter den Linden

▬ Die Prachtstraße „Unter den Linden" führt vom Brandenburger Tor in östlicher Richtung bis zur Schlossbrücke an der Museumsinsel und am Dom. Sie ist eine zentrale Verkehrsachse im Zentrum Berlins und verbindet zahlreiche wichtige Einrichtungen und Sehenswürdigkeiten miteinander. Der ehemalige kurfürstliche Reitweg aus dem 16. Jahrhundert wurde erstmals im Jahr 1647 mit 2000 Nuss- und Lindenbäumen bepflanzt.

⚏ *The magnificent boulevard "Unter den Linden" leads – from the west to the east – from the Brandenburg Gate to the beautiful bridge Schlossbrücke at the Museum Island with the Berlin Cathedral. It is a central main street which connects a number of sights and important facilities. The former elector's riding path dating from the 16th century was planted with 2,000 lime trees and walnut trees for the first time in 1647.*

► Auf dem Mittelstreifen der Prachtstraße

► *On the median strip of the boulevard*

▲ Das Bode-Museum ist eines von fünf bedeutenden Museen auf der Museumsinsel.

▲ *The Bode-Museum is one out of five significant museums on the Museum Island.*

70

Museumsinsel
Museum Island

▬ Als Museumsinsel wird die nördliche Spitze der Spreeinsel im Zentrum Berlins, in unmittelbarer Nähe des Doms, bezeichnet. Auf ihr konzentrieren sich fünf bedeutende Museen, die als kulturelles Ensemble dem Weltkulturerbe der UNESCO angehören: Das Alte Museum, das Neue Museum, das Pergamonmuseum, die Alte Nationalgalerie und das Bode-Museum. Die Museen beherbergen vor allem eine umfangreiche Antikensammlung bis zur römischen Epoche sowie Gemäldesammlungen bis zum 20. Jahrhundert.

▨ *The northern part of the river Spree Island in central Berlin, next to the cathedral, is called Museum Island. No less than five significant museums are concentrated there, which are all world cultural heritage sites: The Alte Museum, the Neue Museum, the Pergamonmuseum, the Alte Nationalgalerie and the Bode-Museum. They mainly house an extensive collection of the ancient world up to the Roman epoch as well as paintings of all times up to the 20th century.*

Gendarmenmarkt
Gendarmenmarkt

▬ Der Gendarmenmarkt, einer der schönsten Plätze Berlins, war ursprünglich als Markt geplant. Zu beiden Seiten des Marktes durften nach 1700 sowohl die lutherische als auch die französisch-reformierte Gemeinde je eine Kirche bauen. Gut 100 Jahre später entstand zwischen beiden Kirchen das königliche Schauspielhaus, das heutige Konzerthaus Berlin, das bis heute den Mittelpunkt dieses einmaligen Ensembles bildet.

🏴󠁧󠁢󠁥󠁮󠁧󠁿 *One of the most beautiful squares of Berlin is the Gendarmenmarkt, which was originally planned as a market place. After 1700, the Lutheran society and the French-Reformed society were allowed to build a church each at both sides of the square. In between, about 100 years later, the royal playhouse was built, which is up to now the centre of this unique ensemble and is currently the Berlin concert hall.*

▲ Das ehemalige königliche Schauspielhaus am Gendarmenmarkt ist heute das Konzerthaus Berlin.

▲ *The former royal playhouse at the square Gendarmenmarkt is now the Berlin concert hall.*

Nikolaiviertel
Nikolaiviertel

▬ Die Kirche St. Nikolai im Bezirk Mitte wurde von 1220 bis 1230 erbaut und ist damit das älteste Bauwerk Berlins. Rund um diese Kirche entwickelte sich die Stadt. Das Nikolaiviertel präsentiert sich heute als Ensemble aus neuen und historischen Gebäuden, die zum Teil auch durch die Zeichnungen von Heinrich Zille bekannt sind. Das Nikolaiviertel ist ein Anziehungspunkt für Touristen, die in Ruhe spazieren, einkaufen oder einfach nur gemütlich in einem Café sitzen wollen.

🏴󠁧󠁢󠁥󠁮󠁧󠁿 *The church Nikolaikirche in the Berlin district Mitte was built from 1220 through 1230. It is the oldest building of the city. The town of Berlin grew around this church. The Nikolaiviertel is today an ensemble of new and historical buildings, which are known from the drawings of Heinrich Zille. The Nikolaiviertel is a favourite place for tourists who like a peaceful walk or shopping tour or like to comfortably sit down for a coffee.*

◄ Blick über die Spree zum Nikolaiviertel

◄ *View across the river Spree into the Nikolai quarter*

Olympiastadion
Olympic Stadium

▬ Das Berliner Olympiastadion befindet sich am West-
rand der Stadt im Bezirk Charlottenburg-Wilmersdorf.
Das 100 000 Zuschauer fassende Stadion wurde anlässlich der Olympischen Sommerspiele 1936 am 1. August
desselben Jahres eingeweiht. In den Jahren 2000 bis
2004 wurde das Olympiastadion für die Fußball-Welt-
meisterschaft 2006 grundlegend modernisiert. Dabei
konnten etwa 70 Prozent der historischen Bausubstanz
erhalten werden – eine Vorgabe des Denkmalschutzes.

※ *The Berlin Olympic Stadium is in the western district
Charlottenburg-Wilmersdorf. It was built for the 1936
Olympic Games and can take up to 100,000 visitors. From
2000 through 2004, the Olympic Stadium was modernized
and prepared for the 2006 soccer world championships.
By request of the protectors of historical monuments, about
70 percent of the historical structure could be preserved.*

▼ Auf Wunsch des Fußballclubs Hertha BSC, aber zum Missfallen
des Denkmalschutzes, wurde das Stadion mit einer blauen Tartan-
bahn ausgestattet.

72

▼ *On request of the soccer club Hertha BSC, the stadion has been
equipped with a blue tartan track.*

KaDeWe
KaDeWe

▬ Das Kaufhaus des Westens (KaDeWe) ist das größte Warenhaus auf dem europäischen Kontinent. Es befindet sich in der Tauentzienstraße, der östlichen Verlängerung des Kurfürstendamms. Gegründet wurde das Kaufhaus des Westens im Jahr 1907, nachdem die Stadtteile Tiergarten, Charlottenburg und Wilmersdorf im Sprachgebrauch unter der Bezeichnung „Neuer Westen" zusammengefasst wurden.

🇬🇧 *The largest department store on the European continent is the so-called Kaufhaus des Westens (KaDeWe). It is located in the Tauentzienstraße east of the Kurfürstendamm. The department store was founded in 1907, after by linguistic usage the Berlin districts Tiergarten, Charlottenburg and Wilmersdorf had been put together under the name "New West". So it was the "department store of the new west".*

◄ Das KaDeWe vereint viele kleine Fachgeschäfte unter einem Dach.

◄ *The KaDeWe unites many small shops under one roof.*

Friedrichstraße
Friedrichstraße

▬ Nicht weit vom Brandenburger Tor kreuzen sich der Boulevard „Unter den Linden" und die Friedrichstraße, ehemals eine der verkehrsreichsten Straßen Berlins, die während der Teilung jegliche Bedeutung verloren hatte. Nach 1990 begann der Neuaufbau der Friedrichstraße mit zahlreichen Boutiquen, Kaufhäusern, Banken und Restaurants. Im nördlichen Abschnitt der Straße liegt der berühmte Friedrichstadtpalast, ein Revuetheater.

🇬🇧 *Not far from the Brandenburg Gate, the boulevard Unter den Linden crosses the Friedrichstraße, which was in former times one of the busiest streets in Berlin, but was without any significance as long as Berlin was divided. From 1990 the street was reconstructed and got numerous boutiques, banks and restaurants. In the northern part of the street is the famous revue theatre Friedrichstadtpalast.*

▲ Während der Teilung Berlins war der Checkpoint Charlie einer der wichtigsten Übergänge vom Westen in den Osten.

▲ *As long as Berlin was divided, Checkpoint Charlie was one of the major gates from West to East Berlin.*

Sachsen-Anhalt
Saxony-Anhalt

Teufelskanzel und Hexenaltar auf dem Brocken im Harz

On the top of the mountain Brocken with its rocks called Teufelskanzel ("Devil's Pulpit") and Hexenaltar ("Witch's Altar")

74

Lage:	in der nordöstlichen Mitte Deutschlands
Fläche:	20 446 km²
Einwohner:	2,4 Millionen
Landeshauptstadt:	Magdeburg
Position:	*in the north-eastern middle of Germany*
Area:	*7900 sq miles*
Inhabitants:	*2.4 million*
Capital:	*Magdeburg*

Magdeburg

Sachsen-Anhalt liegt inmitten der Bundesrepublik und hat vier andere Bundesländer – Niedersachsen, Brandenburg, Sachsen und Thüringen – als Nachbarn. Im Westen teilt es sich mit Niedersachsen den Harz, dessen höchster Gipfel, der 1141 m hohe Brocken, dicht an der Grenze zum Nachbarland steht. Im Norden wird Sachsen-Anhalt vom Flachland der Norddeutschen Tiefebene geprägt.

Das Gebiet des heutigen Sachsen-Anhalt war im frühen Mittelalter einer der kulturellen und politischen Schwerpunkte im deutschsprachigen Raum. Kaum ein anderes Bundesland weist eine derart hohe Dichte an UNESCO-Weltkulturerben auf wie Sachsen-Anhalt.

75

Saxony-Anhalt is in the middle of the Federal Republic and has four other states as neighbours: Lower Saxony, Brandenburg, Saxony and Thuringia. In the west, it shares with Lower Saxony the low mountain area Harz, the highest peak of which – the 3,743-feet high Brocken – is close to the border. The northern part of Saxony-Anhalt is characterized by the flat Northern European Lowlands.

In the early Middle Ages, the region was a cultural and political centre of the German speaking area. The density of cultural world heritage sites is not reached by any other German state.

Magdeburg
Magdeburg

Landeshauptstadt von Sachsen-Anhalt	
Fläche:	200 km²
Einwohner:	230 000
Capital of Saxony-Anhalt	
Area:	*77 sq miles*
Inhabitants:	*230,000*

► Der Jahrtausendturm im Elbauenpark war 1999 das Wahrzeichen der Bundesgartenschau.

► *The Millennium Tower located in the park Elbauenpark was the symbol of the 1999 German Federal Horticulture Show.*

◄ Blick von der Elbe auf den Dom von Magdeburg, das älteste gotische Bauwerk auf deut-
schem Boden

◄ *View from the river Elbe to the cathedral of
Magdeburg which is the oldest Gothic building
in Germany*

▬ Magdeburg liegt an einer Stelle der Elbe, wo der Fluss
in der Frühgeschichte leicht überquert werden konnte.
Bereits vor rund 15 000 Jahren haben sich hier Menschen
angesiedelt. Die Stadtgeschichte begann vor etwa 1200
Jahren zur Zeit Kaiser Karls des Großen. Der rege Handel
im günstig gelegenen Magdeburg bescherte der Stadt
im Jahr 1035 den offiziellen Titel und die Rechte einer
Messestadt.

Nach der Wiedervereinigung Deutschlands 1990 wurde
Magdeburg in einer knappen Abstimmung des ersten
Landtags zwischen Magdeburg und Halle zur neuen Lan-
deshauptstadt bestimmt. Umfangreiche Sanierungen und
Neubauten haben seitdem das in DDR-Zeiten stark gelit-
tene Stadtbild wesentlich aufgewertet.

Zu den Neubauten gehört auch die „Grüne Zitadelle",
ein von dem österreichischen Künstler Friedensreich
Hundertwasser entworfenes Gebäude in unmittelbarer
Nähe des Domplatzes, das 2005 fertiggestellt wurde.

⬛ *Magdeburg is on the banks of the river Elbe at a
place where in former times the river could easily be
crossed. First settlements took place about 15,000 years
ago. The history of the town started under Emperor
Charlemagne about 1,200 years ago. Due to the
favourable strategic location of the town, Magdeburg
prospered and in 1035 received the official title and
the rights of a trade fair city.*

*In 1990, after the reunification of Germany, Magde-
burg was voted for the new capital of Saxony-Anhalt.
Since that time, major reconstructions and new buildings have helped to significantly improve the appearance of the city, which was in a very bad shape in
times of the GDR.*

*One of the new buildings is the so-called Green Citadel
designed by the Austrian artist Friedensreich Hundertwasser. The building is close to the cathedral and was
finished in 2005.*

▼ Das Bauhausgebäude in Dessau wurde
1925/26 nach Entwürfen von Walter Gropius errichtet.

▼ *The Dessau Bauhaus building designed by
Walter Gropius was constructed in 1925/26.*

77

Dessau
Dessau

▬ Dessau – etwa 60 km südöstlich von Magdeburg – ist
die drittgrößte Stadt des Landes Sachsen-Anhalt. Die Lage
an der Mündung des Flusses Mulde in die Elbe ließ die
Stadt schon im 13. Jahrhundert zu einer wichtigen Handelsstadt und später zur Residenzstadt des Herzogtums
Anhalt-Dessau werden. In der Neuzeit wurde Dessau durch
den Architekten Walter Gropius berühmt, der hier die
Kunst-, Design- und Architekturschule „Bauhaus" schuf,
die für die moderne Architektur richtungsweisend wurde.

⬛ *The town of Dessau – about 37 miles south-east of
Magdeburg – is the third largest town of Saxony-Anhalt.
The location, where the river Mulde joins the river Elbe, is
the reason why Dessau was an important trading town already in the 13th century and became the residence of the
duchy of Anhalt-Dessau. In the 20th century, Dessau became famous when the architect Walter Gropius established his art and design school "Bauhaus", which was
pointing the way of modern architecture.*

Halle
Halle

▬ Halle an der Saale ist mit 230 000 Einwohnern die bevölkerungsreichste Stadt in Sachsen-Anhalt. Die Stadt hat ihren frühen Wohlstand und die Mitgliedschaft in der Hanse (seit 1281) einer geologisch günstig gelegenen Salzquelle zu verdanken. Das Wahrzeichen von Halle ist der spätgotische, freistehende Rote Turm auf dem Marktplatz. Er ist der Glockenturm der Marktkirche Unser Lieben Frauen.

▓ *Halle on the banks of the river Saale is the largest city in Saxony-Anhalt and has 230,000 inhabitants. The town became a member of the Hanseatic League in 1281 and prospered well thanks to a salt mine in a favourable geologic location. The symbol of Halle is the Gothic freestanding Rote Turm (Red Tower) at the market square. It is the bell tower of the church Unser Lieben Frauen.*

➤ Der Marktplatz mit dem Roten Turm und der Marktkirche im Hintergrund

➤ *The market square with the freestanding Red Tower and the church in the background*

Wittenberg
Wittenberg

▬ Die Lutherstadt Wittenberg liegt östlich von Dessau an der Elbe. Hier nahm die Reformation Martin Luthers ihren Anfang. Das Lutherhaus, das Haus des Philipp Melanchthon, die Stadt- und die Schlosskirche sind als Luthergedenkstätten seit 1996 Teil des Weltkulturerbes der UNESCO. Auch Lucas Cranach der Ältere, ein enger Freund der Familie Luthers, wirkte hier als Maler der deutschen Reformation.

▓ *The town of Wittenberg on the banks of the river Elbe, east of Dessau, is named Lutherstadt after Martin Luther, who started his Reformation from here. The house of Luther, the house of Philipp Melanchthon as well as the churches are cultural world heritage sites since 1996. Also the artist Lucas Cranach the Elder, a near friend of the Luther family, worked here as a painter of the German Reformation.*

◄ Das Martin-Luther-Denkmal wurde im Jahr 1821 enthüllt.

◄ *The Martin Luther monument is from 1821.*

Quedlinburg
Quedlinburg

🇩🇪 Etwa 50 km südwestlich von Magdeburg liegt die Stadt Quedlinburg. Sie hat zwar nur 22 000 Einwohner, beherbergt aber in ihrer historischen Altstadt mit ihren verwinkelten Gassen rund 1200 Fachwerkhäuser aus sechs Jahrhunderten. Vom 10. bis zum 12. Jahrhundert war Quedlinburg Königspfalz. Die Altstadt ist seit 1994 Weltkulturerbe und gleichzeitig das größte Flächendenkmal in Deutschland.

🇬🇧 *The town of Quedlinburg is about 30 miles south-west of Magdeburg. It has only 22,000 inhabitants, but 1,200 half-timbered houses from six centuries in the winding narrow streets of its historical centre. From the 10th to the 12th century Quedlinburg was a royal palatinate. The historical town is a cultural world heritage site since 1994 and is the largest cultural monument in Germany.*

► Die beeindruckende Altstadt von Quedlinburg

► *The impressive historical town centre of Quedlinburg*

▲ Hoch über der Stadt thront Schloss Wernigerode.

▲ *High above the city the castle of Wernigerode is enthroned.*

Wernigerode
Wernigerode

🇩🇪 Die Stadt Wernigerode liegt am Fuße des Brocken im Harz in bis zu 440 m Höhe über dem Meeresspiegel. Das Wernigeroder Schloss oberhalb der fast 800 Jahre alten Stadt ist schon aus der Ferne zu sehen. Eine besondere Attraktion für Touristen ist eine Schmalspurbahn, die zuerst unter dem Namen Harzquerbahn und dann als Brockenbahn auf den 1141 m hohen Gipfel des Brocken führt.

🇬🇧 *The town of Wernigerode is located at an altitude of 1,440 feet, at the foot of the Harz Mountain "Brocken". The castle of Wernigerode, which overlooks the 800 year old town, can be seen from a distance. A special attraction for tourists is the narrow-gauge railway (named Harzquerbahn and Brockenbahn), which leads to the top of the 3,743-feet Brocken.*

Gartenreich Dessau-Wörlitz
Wörlitz Park

▬ An den östlichen Stadtrand von Dessau schließt sich das Dessau-Wörlitzer Gartenreich an. Es ist eine Kulturlandschaft mit einigen bedeutenden Bauwerken und Landschaftsparks nach englischem Vorbild. Die als Biosphärenreservat des UNESCO-Welterbes eingestufte Fläche von 142 km² wird an mehreren Stellen von der Elbe durchflossen. Das Gartenreich umfasst eine Reihe von Schlössern, unter anderem die Schlösser Luisium, Mosigkau (hier ist auch eine Gemäldegalerie untergebracht), Oranienbaum und Wörlitz.

🇬🇧 *At the eastern town boundary of Dessau, the Wörlitz Park begins. It is an English-style cultural landscape with a number of important buildings. The river Elbe runs through several parts of the area, which is 55 sq miles and is classified as a World Biosphere Reserve. Within the park area are some castles and palaces. Among them are the palaces Luisium, Mosigkau (with an art gallery), Oranienbaum and Wörlitz.*

❚ Schloss Wörlitz wurde von 1769 bis 1773 erbaut.

❚ *The palace Schloss Wörlitz was constructed from 1769 to 1773.*

Burg Querfurt
Querfurt Castle

▬ Die Burg der „Edlen Herren von Querfurt" ist eine der ältesten und größten mittelalterlichen Burgen in Deutschland. Die ältesten Reste an Steingebäuden stammen aus dem 10. Jahrhundert. Im 12. Jahrhundert entstand der wehrhafte Turm „Dicker Heinrich" und kurz darauf die Burgkirche. Die Burg ist von zwei starken Ringmauern umgeben. Sie ist zum Großteil für die Öffentlichkeit zugänglich und gastronomisch bewirtschaftet.

🇬🇧 *The castle of the "nobles of Querfurt" is one of the oldest and largest medieval castles in Germany. Some stone fragments are from the 10th century. The so-called Dicker Heinrich (Fat Henry) is a fortified tower, which was built in the 12th century – as well as the church. The castle is completely surrounded by two strong walls. Most parts are opened for the public and also offer service.*

◄ Blick auf Querfurt und seine mittelalterliche Burg

◄ *View to the town and the medieval castle of Querfurt*

Mittellandkanal
Midland Canal

▬ Der Mittellandkanal ist eine über 300 km lange Wasserstraße, die eine Verbindung zwischen dem Rhein im Westen und der Oder im Osten herstellt. Seit der Eröffnung des Wasserstraßenkreuzes Magdeburg im Jahr 2003 überquert der Kanal die Elbe über eine 900 m lange Kanalbrücke, wird dann bei der Schleuse Hohenwarthe um 19 m abgesenkt und in den Elbe-Havel-Kanal übergeleitet.

🇬🇧 *The Midland Canal is a waterway of 190 miles, which connects the river Rhine in the west with the river Oder in the east. In 2003, the 3,000-feet Magdeburg Water Bridge was opened, which lets the canal cross the river Elbe at a height of 60 feet above Elbe level. Nearby, at Hohenwarthe, a lock connects the Midland Canal with the Elbe-Havel Canal.*

► Das Wasserstraßenkreuz Magdeburg wurde am 10. Oktober 2003 eröffnet.

► *The waterway junction Magdeburg was opened on October 10, 2003.*

Nordrhein-Westfalen
North Rhine-Westphalia

Das Sauerland bei Oberarbach

Sauerland close to the town of Oberarbach

82

Lage:	im Westen Deutschlands, an die Niederlande und an Belgien angrenzend
Fläche:	34 000 km²
Einwohner:	18 Millionen
Landeshauptstadt:	Düsseldorf
Position:	*in the West of Germany, next to the Netherlands and Belgium*
Area:	*13,130 sq miles*
Inhabitants:	*18 million*
Capital:	*Düsseldorf*

Nordrhein-Westfalen (Kurzform: NRW) ist das bevölkerungsreichste und – von den Stadtstaaten abgesehen – das am dichtesten besiedelte Bundesland. Hinter der politischen Einheit NRW verbergen sich tatsächlich drei verschiedene Landesteile, die sich kulturell und mundartlich voneinander unterscheiden: das nördliche Rheinland (Niederrhein), das mittlere Rheinland im Süden des Bundeslandes und Westfalen mit niedersächsischem Einschlag.

Nordrhein-Westfalen ist im Norden geprägt durch das Westfälische Tiefland. Weiter südlich finden sich Hügellandschaften, die als Mittelgebirge Höhen von 500 bis 800 m erreichen. Im Zentrum Nordrhein-Westfalens liegt das Ruhrgebiet, der größte Ballungsraum Deutschlands.

North Rhine-Westphalia (abbreviated: NRW) is – apart from the city states – the most densely populated state of the Federal Republic. The political state NRW actually consists of three distinct regions, which differ from each other in culture as well as in dialect: the North Rhineland (lower Rhine valley), the Middle Rhineland in the South of the state and Westphalia as the eastern part of the land next to Lower Saxony.

The north of North Rhine-Westphalia is characterized by lowland. To the south there are hilly landscapes and low mountain areas in the top altitude range of 1,600 to 2,000 feet. The Ruhr valley in the centre of North Rhine-Westphalia is the largest urban centre in Germany.

Düsseldorf
Düsseldorf

Landeshauptstadt von Nordrhein-Westfalen	
Fläche:	217 km²
Einwohner:	578 000
Capital of North Rhine-Westphalia	
Area:	*84 sq miles*
Inhabitants:	*578,000*

► Wo früher Autos fuhren, verbindet heute eine 2 km lange Uferpromenade die historische Altstadt mit dem modernen Medienhafen.

► *More than one mile of a busy road has been changed into a promenade along the Rhine which connects now the historical city centre to the modern Media Port.*

◄ Blick über den Rhein zum Düsseldorfer Fernsehturm. Der Bürokomplex daneben entstand auf ehemaligem Hafengelände und wird „Medienhafen" genannt.

◄ *View across the river Rhine. The office buildings next to the TV tower were built on the former port area and are called "Media Port".*

🇩🇪 Die Landeshauptstadt ist die drittgrößte Stadt des Bundeslandes. Das „Dorf an der Düssel" (an deren Mündung in den Rhein) wurde 1288 zur Stadt erhoben. In seiner wechselvollen Geschichte stand die Stadt von 1795 bis 1801 unter französischer Herrschaft, kam dann kurzzeitig zu Bayern und schließlich 1815 zu Preußen. Mit dem Beginn der Industrialisierung im 19. Jahrhundert wuchs die Bevölkerung Düsseldorfs stark an.

Zahlreiche internationale Industrie- und Wirtschaftsunternehmen haben ihren Sitz in Düsseldorf, das auch eine bedeutende Messestadt ist – unter anderem findet hier die größte Modemesse der Welt statt.

Düsseldorf ist auch ein wichtiges Zentrum der Kunst. Im 19. Jahrhundert hatte die Düsseldorfer Malerschule großen Einfluss auf die zeitgenössische Malerei. Und in der zweiten Hälfte 20. Jahrhunderts prägten Joseph Beuys und seine Schüler von der Kunstakademie Düsseldorf die internationale Kunstszene.

🇬🇧 *The capital is the third largest city of the state. The original village developed where the river Düssel joins the river Rhine and received its municipal rights in 1288. During its varied history the town was under French rule from 1795 to 1801, then for a short time under Bavarian rule and finally became a part of Prussia in 1815. Due to the industrialization in the 19th century, the population of Düsseldorf increased rapidly.*

Many international enterprises have their headquarters in Düsseldorf, which is an important exhibition centre with the largest fashion exhibition of the world.

Also, Düsseldorf is a significant centre of the arts. Düsseldorf's school of painting of the 19th century had major influence on the contemporary art. In the second half of the 20th century Joseph Beuys and his students had a forming influence on the international art scene.

▼ Die Zeche Zollverein, ein Weltkulturerbe, ist das wohl bedeutendste Baudenkmal der Schwerindustrie im Ruhrgebiet.

▼ *The coal mine called Zollverein, a world cultural heritage, is probably the most significant industrial monument of the Ruhr valley.*

Essen
Essen

🇩🇪 Die Stadt Essen im Zentrum des Ruhrgebiets zählt etwa ebenso viele Einwohner wie Düsseldorf. Das Gebiet war schon in vorchristlicher Zeit besiedelt. Der Abbau von Bodenschätzen – zunächst Silber, deutlich später Kohle – erfolgte jedoch offenbar erst seit dem 14. Jahrhundert. Heute ist der Kohlebergbau weitgehend zum Erliegen gekommen. Der einstige „Kohlenpott" wandelt sich zu einer sauberen Natur- und Kulturregion. In Anerkennung dessen wurde Essen zur Europäischen Kulturhauptstadt des Jahres 2010 gewählt.

🇬🇧 *The city of Essen is in the centre of the Ruhr valley and has about the same number of inhabitants as Düsseldorf. The region was populated already in pre-Christian times. However, the mining of mineral resources – first of all silver, then coal – apparently did not start until the 14th century. Today, coal mining is largely finished. The area is transforming itself into a clean natural and cultural region. In appreciation of this change, Essen has been voted for European cultural capital of the year 2010.*

Aachen
Aachen

▬ Aachen ist die westlichste Stadt Deutschlands. An den heißen, schwefelhaltigen Quellen der Umgebung siedelten schon Kelten und Römer. Unter Kaiser Karl dem Großen wurde Aachen ein bedeutendes Kurbad. Die von ihm um das Jahr 800 erbaute Pfalzkapelle erhielt später als Aachener Dom die größte frei schwebende Kuppel nördlich der Alpen. Der Marmorthron des Kaisers steht heute noch im Dom.

🇬🇧 *Aachen is the westernmost town of Germany. Celts and Romans already settled near the hot sulphurous springs of the area. Under Emperor Charlemagne, Aachen became a famous spa. His Palatine Chapel, which was built in about 800, was later on expanded to become Aachen Cathedral, which had at the time of construction the largest dome north of the Alps. The emperor's marble throne is still in the cathedral.*

► Im Aachener Dom wurden vom 10. bis zum 16. Jahrhundert 30 deutsche Könige gekrönt.

► *From the 10th to the 16th century, 30 German kings were crowned in Aachen Cathedral.*

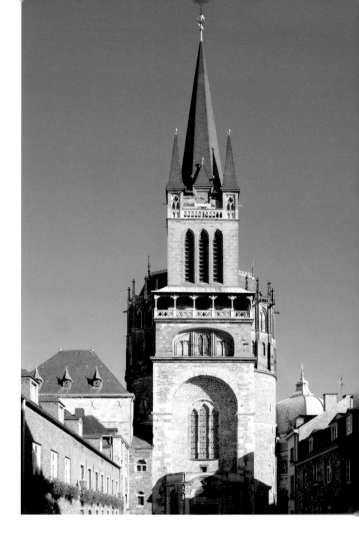

Köln
Cologne

▬ Das 2000 Jahre alte Köln, eine Gründung der Römer, ist die viertgrößte Stadt Deutschlands. Durch die vor kalten Westwinden geschützte Lage am Rhein ist die Innenstadt von Köln der wärmste Ort Deutschlands. Wahrzeichen der Stadt ist der Dom mit den angeblichen Reliquien der Heiligen Drei Könige. Ebenso berühmt ist aber auch der Kölner Karneval, dessen Höhepunkt am Rosenmontag gefeiert wird.

🇬🇧 *The 2,000 year old city of Cologne, founded by the Romans, is the fourth large city of Germany. Its location on the banks of the river Rhine, protected from the west wind, makes Cologne the warmest place in Germany. The symbol of the city is Cologne Cathedral with the Relic Shrine of the Three Kings. A famous event is the Cologne Carnival with its parade which takes place on the Monday preceding Ash Wednesday.*

◄ Der Kölner Dom mit seinen 157 m hohen Türmen ist der größte Kirchenbau der Gotik.

◄ *With its 515 feet high twin towers, Cologne Cathedral is the largest Gothic church.*

Bonn
Bonn

Bonn am Rhein, die Nachbarstadt von Köln, war von 1949 bis 1999 Hauptstadt und Regierungssitz der Bundesrepublik Deutschland. Offiziell beginnt die Geschichte Bonns vor 2000 Jahren als Römersiedlung. Tatsächlich war das Gebiet schon sehr viel früher besiedelt, wie unter anderem eine 14 000 Jahre alte Grabstätte beweist. Unter Napoleon wurde Bonn vorübergehend französisch, fiel dann an Preußen und wurde im 19. Jahrhundert eine bedeutende Universitätsstadt.

Eines der Bonner Wahrzeichen ist das Alte Rathaus, wo Theodor Heuss als soeben gewählter, erster Präsident der Bundesrepublik vor die Bonner trat. Auch Präsidenten anderer Staaten hielten von hier aus Ansprachen: 1962 der französische Staatspräsident Charles de Gaulle, 1963 John F. Kennedy und 1989 der sowjetische Staatschef Michail Gorbatschow. Der vielleicht berühmteste Sohn Bonns ist Ludwig van Beethoven, dessen Denkmal auf dem Münsterplatz steht.

▼ Die Villa Hammerschmidt, erbaut für einen Industriellen des späten 19. Jahrhunderts, wurde 1951 der Amtssitz des Bundespräsidenten.

▼ *The Villa Hammerschmidt, built for a manufacturer of the late 19th century, became in 1951 the residence of the President of the Federal Republic.*

▲ Das Kunstmuseum Bonn hat seinen Schwerpunkt auf die deutsche Kunst des 20. Jahrhunderts gelegt.

▲ *The Bonn Museum of Arts is mainly focussed on German arts of the 20th century.*

Bonn, neighbour city of Cologne, was the capital of the Federal Republic from 1949 to 1999. Officially, its history started as a Roman settlement 2,000 years ago. Actually, the region was settled much earlier, as can been seen from 14,000 year old graves. For a short period, Bonn was ruled by Napoleon before it became a part of Prussia. The University was founded in the early 19th century.

One of the symbols of Bonn is the old town hall, where Theodor Heuss who had just been voted first president of the Federal Republic spoke to the public. Presidents of other nations also held speeches from here: the French president Charles de Gaulle in 1962, the US president John F. Kennedy in 1963, the USSR president Michail Gorbatschow in 1989. Probably the most famous person who was born in Bonn is Ludwig van Beethoven. His monument is located on the square Münsterplatz.

Ruhrgebiet
Ruhr Area

■ Der Name „Ruhrgebiet" bezeichnet eine Region, die mit der Industrialisierung im 19. und 20. Jahrhundert zum größten Ballungsraum in Deutschland mit etwa 5,3 Millionen Einwohnern wurde. Viele Städte sind hier zusammengewachsen, unter anderem die Großstädte Bochum, Bottrop, Dortmund, Duisburg, Essen, Gelsenkirchen, Hagen, Hamm, Herne, Mülheim an der Ruhr, Oberhausen und Recklinghausen.

Im Bereich des Flusses Ruhr lagern große Vorkommen an Steinkohle, wobei die Kohlenflöze in Flussnähe relativ bodennah liegen und nach Norden hin sehr tief absinken. Der Kohlebergbau und die auf Kohle angewiesene Stahlindustrie haben das Bild des Ruhrgebiets entscheidend geprägt.

Nachdem die wirtschaftlich erschließbaren Kohlevorkommen abgebaut sind, ist der Bergbau in den letzten Jahrzehnten fast völlig zum Erliegen gekommen. Im Rahmen eines gewaltigen Strukturwandels entsteht an der Ruhr eine neue Natur- und Kulturlandschaft.

⊞ *The name Ruhr Area means a region which, in the course of the industrialization of the 19th and 20th century, became the largest conurbation in Germany with about 5.3 millions of inhabitants. Numerous towns fused with each other in this area, as did Bochum, Bottrop, Dortmund, Duisburg, Essen, Gelsenkirchen, Hagen, Hamm, Herne, Mülheim an der Ruhr, Oberhausen and Recklinghausen.*

Within the area of the river Ruhr are rich coal deposits. Whereas the coal seams near the river are close to the surface, they sink into the depths towards the north. The coal mining and the dependent steel industry have decisively characterized the face of the Ruhr Area.

After the exploitable coalfields had been mined, the mining almost came to stagnancy. A huge restructuring program is now creating a new natural and cultural landscape.

▼ Riesige Schaufelradbagger fördern Braunkohle. Einige Jahre später wird hier eine Freizeit- und Erholungslandschaft entstehen.

▼ *Huge excavators deliver brown coal. A few years from now, this place will become a leisure and recreation area.*

88

Münsterland
Münsterland

🇩🇪 Im Norden von Nordrhein-Westfalen liegt das Münsterland mit der Stadt Münster als Zentrum. Die weitgehend flache Landschaft wird landwirtschaftlich intensiv genutzt. Daneben ist auch die Pferde- und Viehzucht weit verbreitet. Das Münsterland lässt sich hervorragend mit dem Fahrrad erkunden. An der so genannten Schlösser-Route liegen alle bedeutenden Burgen und Schlösser, darunter auch viele Wasserschlösser.

🇬🇧 *In the north of North Rhine-Westphalia is the region Münsterland with the town of Münster in its centre. The flat landscape is highly productive agricultural land. Besides this, horse breeding and cattle farming are widespread. It is a good idea to explore the Münsterland by bicycle. The so-called Schlösser-Route (castle route) passes all significant castles and places, among them many moated castles.*

▲ Das Wasserschloss Hülshoff ist das Geburtshaus der Dichterin Annette von Droste-Hülshoff, die hier am 10. Januar 1797 geboren wurde.

▲ *The Hülshoff castle, built in water, is the birthplace of the poet Annette von Droste-Hülshoff. She was born on January 10, 1797.*

Teutoburger Wald
Teutoburg Forest

🇩🇪 Östlich von Münster – im Raum Bielefeld und Osnabrück – verläuft der Teutoburger Wald, ein Mittelgebirge mit Erhebungen von etwa 400 m Höhe. Der Teutoburger Wald erlangte Bekanntheit durch die nach ihm benannte Schlacht im Jahr 9 n. Chr., in der der römische Feldherr Varus von den Germanen vernichtend geschlagen wurde. Nach heutigen Erkenntnissen fand die Schlacht jedoch in einiger Entfernung vom Teutoburger Wald statt.

🇬🇧 *East of Münster – in the area of the towns Bielefeld and Osnabrück – is the Teutoburg Forest, a low mountain area with altitudes of up to 1,300 feet. The Teutoburg Forest became well known by the Teutoburg Battle in 9 AD, when the Roman commander Varus was annihilated by German tribes. According to recent findings however, the battle actually took place some distance from the Teutoburg Forest.*

▲ Die so genannten Externsteine im Teutoburger Wald zogen die Menschen schon vor 12 000 Jahren an.

▲ *The so-called Extern Stones in the Teutoburg Forest attracted men already 12,000 years ago.*

Bergisches Land
Bergisches Land

▬ An das südliche Ruhrgebiet grenzt das Bergische Land an, das mit den Städten Wuppertal, Remscheid und Solingen bis an den Kölner Raum heranreicht. In der sehr bergigen und wasserreichen Gegend wurde schon frühzeitig die Wasserkraft für die Metallverarbeitung und die Textilindustrie genutzt. Messer aus Solingen sind in aller Welt bekannt. Eine technische Sehenswürdigkeit ist die Wuppertaler Schwebebahn.

🇬🇧 *Next to the southern Ruhr Area is the region Bergisches Land with its major cities Wuppertal, Remscheid and Solingen. The hilly land with plenty of water enabled very early a water powered metal and textile industry. Solingen is almost synonymous with high quality knives. A technical sight is the Wuppertaler Schwebebahn, a monorail with carriages suspended from a single rail.*

► Seit dem Jahr 1900 ist die Wuppertaler Schwebebahn eines der wichtigsten Verkehrsmittel in der Stadt.

► *Since 1900, the Wuppertaler Schwebebahn has been one of the important traffic systems in the city.*

90

Sauerland
Sauerland

▬ Im Südosten von Nordrhein-Westfalen liegt die Mittelgebirgsregion Sauerland. Die bedeutendsten Berge erreichen eine Höhe von über 800 m. Die ersten Spuren einer Besiedlung stammen aus der Stein- und der Eisenzeit. Allerdings war das Land nie dicht besiedelt. Für den Naturfreund bietet das Sauerland eine Reihe von Naturparks von überregionaler Bedeutung sowie eine Vielzahl von begehbaren Höhlen.

▲ Das Sauerland zählt zu den beliebtesten Ferienregionen im nördlichen Deutschland.

▲ *The Sauerland is one of the most popular holiday regions in northern Germany.*

🇬🇧 *In the south-east of North Rhine-Westphalia is the low mountain area Sauerland. The major mountains have altitudes of more than 2,600 feet. The first signs of settlements are from the Stone Age and the Iron Age. However, the land was never densely populated. The Sauerland offers the nature-lover a number of natural parks of nationwide importance as well as numerous caves which are open to the public.*

Siegerland
Siegerland

🇩🇪 Im Süden von Nordrhein-Westfalen liegen die Stadt Siegen und das umliegende Siegerland. Seit etwa 600 v. Chr. bis in die Mitte des 20. Jahrhunderts wurde hier Eisenerz abgebaut. Die Erzvorkommen sind nach Schätzung von Geologen noch nicht erschöpft. Kulturell und sprachlich orientiert sich das Siegerland an den hessischen und Westerwälder Nachbarn und grenzt sich deutlich vom benachbarten Sauerland ab.

🇬🇧 *In the south of North Rhine-Westphalia is the town of Siegen with its surrounding region Siegerland. Iron ore was mined there from 600 BC to the middle of the 20th century. According to experts, the iron ore deposits are not exhausted yet. With regard to culture and dialect the Siegerland orientates more towards the regions Hesse and Westerwald rather than towards its neighbour Sauerland.*

▲ Die Stadt Freudenberg entstand 1969 aus 17 einzelnen Gemeinden. Ihre Fachwerkhäuser stammen jedoch aus dem 16. Jahrhundert.

▲ *The town of Freudenberg was created in 1969 from no less than 17 single villages. The half-timbered houses, however, are from the 16th century.*

91

Eifel
Eifel

🇩🇪 Südwestlich von Bonn breitet sich das Mittelgebirge der Eifel aus. Nach Westen hin setzt sich die Eifel in den belgischen Ardennen fort. Der Naturpark Eifel im nördlichen Teil ist ein interessantes Ziel für den Naturfreund. Weiter südlich – schon in Rheinland-Pfalz – befindet sich der Nürburgring, die klassische Autorennstrecke, die von vielen Rennfahrern als die schönste der Welt bezeichnet wird.

🇬🇧 *To the south-west of the city of Bonn is the low mountain region Eifel. To the west, the Eifel expands into Belgium where this low mountain area is named Ardennes. The natural park in the northern part of the Eifel is an interesting destination for nature-lovers. In the south, already in Rhineland-Palatinate, is the Nürburgring, the classic race track – for many drivers the most beautiful in the world.*

◄ Die Burg Eltz ist eine der wenigen Burgen, die im Laufe der Jahrhunderte nie zerstört wurden. Ihr Bild zierte die früheren 500-DM-Banknoten.

◄ *The castle Eltz is one of the very few castles which were never destroyed through all the centuries. Its picture was on the former 500 Deutschmark notes.*

Sachsen
Saxony

▼ Die Basteibrücke im Elbsandsteingebirge ist ebenfalls aus Sandstein gebaut.

▼ *The Bastei Bridge in the Elbe Sandstone
Mountains is also made from sandstone.*

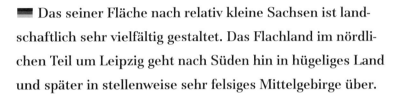

Lage:	östliches Bundesland an der Grenze zu Tschechien und Polen
Fläche:	18 400 km²
Einwohner:	4,2 Millionen
Landeshauptstadt:	Dresden
Position:	*in the east of Germany, next to the Czech Republic and to Poland*
Area:	*7,100 sq miles*
Inhabitants:	*4.2 million*
Capital:	*Dresden*

▬ Das seiner Fläche nach relativ kleine Sachsen ist landschaftlich sehr vielfältig gestaltet. Das Flachland im nördlichen Teil um Leipzig geht nach Süden hin in hügeliges Land und später in stellenweise sehr felsiges Mittelgebirge über.

Das sehr fruchtbare Hügelland gehört zu den ältesten Siedlungs- und Zivilisationsgebieten in Europa. In der Neuzeit führte die Völkerwanderung zuerst germanische und dann slawische Stämme in die Region. Das spätere Sachsen wurde durch das Adelsgeschlecht der Wettiner geprägt, die im Jahr 1089 die Markgrafschaft Meißen übernahmen und bis 1918 den König von Sachsen stellten. Der heutige Freistaat Sachsen wurde 1990 gegründet und erlebt seitdem einen enormen Strukturwandel.

🏴 *The relatively small state of Saxony is a manifold landscape. The lowland in the northern area around Leipzig changes into hilly regions towards the south and turns later on into a very rocky low mountain range.*

The highly productive hilly land is one of the oldest areas of settlement and civilisation within Europe. In the time after Christ the migration of the people at first brought German and then Slavic tribes into the region. The later state of Saxony was characterized by the aristocratic Wettin family, which took over the Meissen Margravate in 1089 and provided the Kings of Saxony until 1918. The current state of Saxony was founded in 1990 and is experiancing a dramatic change of structure.

Dresden
Dresden

Landeshauptstadt von Sachsen	
Fläche:	328 km²
Einwohner:	505 000
Capital of Saxony	
Area:	*127 sq miles*
Inhabitants:	*505,000*

► Über eine Brücke und das prächtige Kronentor gelangt man zum Park des 1719 erbauten Zwingers, einem Festplatz für Turniere und Spiele des sächsischen Adels.

► *A bridge and the great Crown Gate lead to the garden of the Zwinger which was built in 1719 as festival place of the Saxon aristocrats.*

◄ Das Residenzschloss in Dresden ist eines der bedeutendsten Renaissance-Bauwerke in Deutschland.

◄ *The palace Residenzschloss in Dresden is one of the most important Renaissance buildings in Germany.*

Dresden liegt landschaftlich reizvoll am Übergang vom Nordostdeutschen Tiefland zu den östlichen Mittelgebirgen. Die durch Dresden fließende Elbe mit ihren ehemals vier historischen Brücken und die barocke Architektur der Stadt haben Dresden den Beinamen „Elbflorenz" eingetragen. Die größte kulturelle Blüte erlebte das 800 Jahre alte Dresden zu Zeiten Augusts des Starken (1670–1733), unter dessen Herrschaft die wichtigsten Prachtbauten Dresdens entstanden, unter anderem der Zwinger, die berühmte Frauenkirche und Teile des Residenzschlosses.

Die im zweiten Weltkrieg weitgehend zerstörte Stadt wird seit 1990 erfolgreich wiederaufgebaut. Der Neubau der Frauenkirche konnte im Jahr 2005 eingeweiht werden. Das Schloss und der Zwinger, die bedeutende Kunstsammlungen beherbergen, sind in Teilen wiedereröffnet.

The charming location of Dresden is where the north-east German lowland turns into the eastern low mountain areas. The river Elbe, which runs through Dresden, and the formerly four historical bridges as well as the Baroque architecture of the city, gave Dresden the name "Elbflorenz" ("Florence of the Elbe"). The cultural prime time of the 800 years old town was under the rule of August the Strong (1670–1733). The most important magnificent buildings were built in his time, among others the palace Zwinger, the church Frauenkirche and parts of the palace Residenzschloss.

The city which was almost completely destroyed during World War II is being reconstructed since 1990. The rebuilt Frauenkirche was officially opened in 2005. The palace and the Zwinger with their significant collections of art are partly reopened.

▼ Die Semperoper ist nach ihrem Baumeister Manfred Semper benannt, der das berühmte Bauwerk im Jahr 1878 vollendete.

▼ *The opera house Semperoper is named after its architect Manfred Semper, who finished the famous building in 1878.*

95

■ Leipzig ist – knapp vor Dresden – die bevölkerungsreichste Stadt in Sachsen und seit dem Mittelalter ein wichtiges Handelszentrum. Leipzigs Tradition als bedeutender Messestandort geht auf das Jahr 1190 zurück – das heutige Messezentrum ist ausgesprochen modern. Die 1409 gegründete Universität Leipzig ist eine der ältesten in Deutschland und die älteste Tageszeitung der Welt von 1650 stammt ebenfalls aus Leipzig.

Die Thomaskirche war die Wirkungsstätte von Johann Sebastian Bach, dessen Denkmal vor der Kirche steht. Die Nikolaikirche wurde zum Ausgangspunkt der „Montagsdemonstrationen", die zur Wiedervereinigung Deutschlands beitrugen. Der sagenumwobene Auerbachs Keller beeindruckte den Studenten Johann Wolfgang Goethe so sehr, dass er den Ort in sein Drama „Faust" aufnahm. Der 1915 eröffnete Leipziger Hauptbahnhof ist mit seiner fast 300 m breiten Fassade – und seit 1997 mit einem Einkaufszentrum auf drei Ebenen – der größte Kopfbahnhof Europas.

❚ Das neue Gewandthaus in Leipzig, das in den Jahren 1977 bis 1981 erbaut wurde. Das ursprüngliche Gebäude wurde als Zeughaus im Jahr 1498 errichtet.

❚ *The new Gewandthaus in Leipzig which was built from 1977 to 1981. The original building was constructed in 1498 as an arsenal.*

⌘ *Leipzig is – narrowly before Dresden – the most populated city of Saxony. Since the Middle Ages, Leipzig has been an important trading centre. Its tradition as an exhibition centre dates back to 1190. The exhibition area of today is absolutely up-to-date. The Leipzig University was founded in 1409 and is one of the oldest universities in Germany. The world's oldest daily newspaper from 1650 was published in Leipzig.*

The church of St. Thomas was the workplace of Johann Sebastian Bach, whose monument is in front of the church. The church of St. Nicholas (Nikolaikirche) was the starting point of the so-called "Monday demonstrations", which contributed to the reunification of Germany. As a student, Johann Wolfgang Goethe was so impressed by the legendary restaurant Auerbachs Keller that he took this place into his drama "Faust". The Leipzig central railway station was opened in 1915. With its 960-foot-long facade, it is one of the largest stations in Europe.

▲ Meißen ist berühmt für sein Hand be-
maltes Meissener Porzellan®, hier z. B.
das Dekor „Weiße Rose mit Purpurkern".

▲ Meißen is famous for its handmade
china products as for example the de-
cor "White rose with purple centre".

Meißen
Meißen

■ Etwa 25 km nordwestlich von Dresden liegt die kleine Stadt
Meißen, deren Name weltberühmt wurde, nachdem August der
Starke per Dekret vom 23. Januar 1710 die „Königlich-Polnische
und Kurfürstlich-Sächsische Porzellanmanufaktur" gegründet hatte.
Dem Alchemisten Johann Friedrich Böttger war die befohlene Her-
stellung von Gold missglückt. So wurde er ins Gefängnis gesteckt
und mehr oder weniger gezwungen, sich an der experimentellen
Entwicklung von Porzellan zu beteiligen. Schließlich gelang es, das
erste weiße Hartporzellan in Europa herzustellen. Ab 1710 wurde
Porzellan unter Böttgers Leitung fabrikmäßig hergestellt.

Meißen liegt mit seiner sehenswerten historischen Innenstadt an
der Elbe und kann unter anderem von Dresden aus per Schiff erreicht werden. Die wichtigste Sehenswürdigkeit ist natürlich die
Porzellan-Manufaktur mit dem Porzellan-Museum und dessen
Schauwerkstätten.

※ *About 15 miles north-west of Dresden is the
small town Meißen which became famous all over
the world after August the Strong on January 23,
1710 had ordered the founding of the china manu-
factory "Königlich-Polnische und Kurfürstlich-Sächsische Porzellanmanufaktur" (KPM). The alchemist
Johann Friedrich Böttger had not been successful in
producing gold. He was taken into prison and
forced to participate in the development of porcelain. Finally, he succeeded in producing Europe's
first white china. From 1710, Böttger was in charge
of the series production of china.*

*The historical centre of Meißen, which is on the
banks of the river Elbe, is worth seeing. It can be
reached by ship from Dresden. The most important
sights are of course the china factory with its china
museum and the studios.*

Chemnitz
Chemnitz

Chemnitz liegt am Nordrand des Erzgebirges südwestlich von Dresden. Die Stadt entstand nach der Gründung eines Benediktinerklosters im Jahr 1136, wurde schon im Mittelalter ein wichtiges Wirtschaftszentrum und ab dem 17. Jahrhundert ein bedeutender Standort der Textilindustrie. Zu Zeiten der DDR hatte man Chemnitz in „Karl-Marx-Stadt" umbenannt. Im Jahr 1990 sprachen sich jedoch die Bürger für den alten Namen aus.

The city of Chemnitz is located at the northern edge of the Erzgebirge (Ore Mountains), south-west of Dresden. The town developed around a Benedictine monastery which was founded in 1136. Chemnitz became an important commercial town in the Middle Ages and – from the 17th century – a major centre of the upcoming textile industry. Under the rule of the GDR the city had been named "Karl-Marx-Stadt", but was renamed in 1990.

► Karl-Marx-Denkmal. Zur Zeit der DDR war Chemnitz in Karl-Marx-Stadt umbenannt worden.

► *Karl Marx monument. During the period of the GDR, Chemnitz had been named Karl-Marx-City.*

98

Zittau
Zittau

Die Stadt Zittau liegt im äußersten Südosten Sachsens in unmittelbarer Nähe des Dreiländerecks Deutschland-Polen-Tschechien. Zittau stand seit dem 13. Jahrhundert unter mehrfach wechselnder Herrschaft, bis es 1635 zu Sachsen kam und nicht zuletzt durch seinen Leinwandhandel zu erheblichem Reichtum kam. Die Osterweiterung der Europäischen Union könnte der Grenzstadt Zittau neue Impulse geben.

The town of Zittau is in the very south-east of Saxony, next to the point where the countries Germany, Poland and the Czech Republic meet. Since the 13th century, Zittau was under varying rules, until it finally became a part of Saxony and prospered very well by trading with linen. The opening of the borders to the East may give the border town new impetus.

◄ Das 1845 erbaute Rathaus von Zittau in der Abendsonne

◄ *The town hall of Zittau, built in 1845, during sunset*

Zwickau
Zwickau

Im Westen des Freistaates Sachsen und wie Chemnitz am Nordrand des Erzgebirges liegt die Stadt Zwickau, auf dessen Gebiet im 7. Jahrhundert slawische Stämme siedelten. Im 10. Jahrhundert wanderten germanische Siedler ein. Seit dem Mittelalter wird in Zwickau Steinkohle abgebaut, deren Flöze teilweise bis an die Erdoberfläche reichen. Erst Ende der 1970er-Jahre wurden die letzten Steinkohlegruben in der Stadt geschlossen.

Im Jahr 1904 gründete August Horch in Zwickau sein erstes Automobilwerk „Horch" und einige Jahre später die „Audi"-Werke. („Audi" ist das lateinische Wort für die Aufforderung „Horch!".) Seit dieser Zeit wurden in Zwickau immer Autos gebaut. Von 1957 bis 1991 war dies der DDR-Volkswagen „Trabant". Danach übernahm die Volkswagen Sachsen GmbH die Produktion von Automobilen.

Der wohl bedeutendste Zwickauer ist der 1810 geborene Komponist Robert Schumann. Sein Geburtshaus steht am Hauptmarkt.

Zwickau is in the west of the state of Saxony and – like Chemnitz – at the northern edge of the Ore Mountains. During the 7th century, Slavic tribes settled there, but were replaced by German tribes in the 10th century. From the Middle Ages onwards, hard coal has been mined in Zwickau. At some places, the coal seams reach up to the surface of the earth. The last coal mine of the town was closed only in the late 1970s.

In 1904, August Horch established in Zwickau his first motorcar factory named "Horch" – and some years later the factory "Audi" ("Audi" is the Latin word of the German word "horch" which means the request "listen to me!"). Since that time, motorcars have been built in Zwickau. From 1957 to 1991 the GDR standard car "Trabant" was built there.

Probably the most significant citizen of Zwickau is the composer Robert Schumann who was born in 1810. His birth house is at the square Hauptmarkt.

▼ Das August Horch Museum zeigt alle seit 1904 in Zwickau produzierten Automobile.

▼ *The August Horch Museum shows all cars which were produced in Zwickau since 1904.*

■ Etwa 25 km südlich von Dresden im Erzgebirge liegt der kleine, nur 4500 Einwohner zählende Ort Glashütte. Seit dem späten Mittelalter wurde hier Silbererz abgebaut. Zu Beginn des 19. Jahrhunderts waren die Erzlagerstätten jedoch weitgehend erschöpft. Um die wirtschaftliche Lage der Bevölkerung zu verbessern, finanzierte die königlich-sächsische Regierung die Ansiedlung von Handwerkern. Im Jahr 1845 ließ sich der Sachse Ferdinand Adolph Lange als erster Uhrmachermeister in Glashütte nieder. Er erhielt vom Staat 7000 Taler und bildete Uhrmacher aus. Dreißig Jahre später war die Uhrenindustrie das wirtschaftliche Rückgrat der Stadt.

Nach dem Zweiten Weltkrieg wurde die Uhrenindustrie in Glashütte verstaatlicht. Seit 1990 erleben die Nachfolger von Adolph Lange jedoch einen unvergleichlichen Aufschwung. Uhren aus Glashütte gehören heute in Qualität, Prestige und Preis zur absoluten Weltspitze.

■ *About 15 miles south of Dresden is an Ore Mountains village with only 4,500 inhabitants: Glashütte. From the late Middle Ages to the early 19th century the people lived from silver mining. Then the deposits were exhausted. In order to improve the economical situation, the royal Saxon government financed the settlement of craftsmen there. In 1845, the first watchmaker, Ferdinand Adolph Lange, equipped with 7,000 Thaler (silver coins), settled in Glashütte. Thirty years later, the watch industry had become the economic backbone of the town.*

After World War II the Glashütte watch industry was nationalized and declined. Since 1990 however, the successors of Adolph Lange are experiencing an incomparable upturn. Today's watches from Glashütte are top in the world in terms of quality, prestige – and price.

❚ In Glashütte wird beste handwerkliche Kunst gepflegt. Ruhe und Konzentration sind die Voraussetzung für perfekte Meisterwerke.

❚ *Best craftsmanship in Glashütte. Patience and concentration are mandatory in order to get perfect masterpieces.*

Radebeul
Radebeul

🔲 Unmittelbar an Dresden angrenzend – flussabwärts an der Elbe – liegt Radebeul. An dem nach Süden geneigten Elbeufer herrscht ein derart mildes Klima, dass in und um Radebeul an der Sächsischen Weinstraße Wein angebaut wird. Hier befindet sich mit 350 ha das kleinste und nordöstlichste Weinbaugebiet Deutschlands. Neben den typischen deutschen Trauben wird auch eine Besonderheit, der Goldriesling, angebaut.

🏴󠁧󠁢󠁥󠁮󠁧󠁿 *Next to Dresden, down the river Elbe, is the town of Radebeul. The banks of the river, which are oriented towards the south, enjoy such a very mild climate, that the area around Radebeul – the Saxon Wine Route – is used for viniculture. It is the smallest and most north-easternly wine growing region of Germany. Besides the typical German grapes, a speciality, the Goldriesling, is cultivated.*

◄ Das 1622 erbaute traditionsreiche Spitzhaus in den Weinbergen wurde 1902 zu einem Restaurant umgebaut.

◄ *The traditional Spitzhaus of 1622 in the vineyards was changed into a restaurant in 1902.*

Elbsandsteingebirge
Elbe Sandstone Mountains

🔲 Das Elbsandsteingebirge ist ein Mittelgebirge am Oberlauf der Elbe in Deutschland und zu einem kleinen Teil in Tschechien. Durch Erosion des weichen Sandsteins ist hier ein stark zerklüftetes Felsengebirge entstanden, das auf engstem Raum eine außerordentliche Artenvielfalt an Pflanzen hervorgebracht hat. Große Teile des Gebirges, so der Nationalpark Sächsische Schweiz, stehen unter Naturschutz.

🏴󠁧󠁢󠁥󠁮󠁧󠁿 *Elbe Sandstone Mountains is a low mountain range in the upper reaches of the river Elbe, expanding to a smaller part into the Czech Republic. By erosion, soft sandstone has been turned into deeply fissured rocks, which enabled a huge variety of plants in a small area. A major part of the mountain area is protected, especially the national park Sächsische Schweiz (Saxon Switzerland).*

► Mit nur 500 Einwohnern auf beiden Seiten der Elbe ist Rathen der kleinste Kurort in Deutschland. Eine historische Seilfähre verbindet beide Ortsteile.

► *With only 500 inhabitants on both banks of the Elbe, the village of Rathen is the smallest spa in Germany. A historical Elbe ferry connects both parts of the village.*

Bautzen
Bautzen

▬ Die Stadt Bautzen liegt 50 km östlich von Dresden an der Spree. Ihren heutigen Namen erhielt die Stadt erst 1868. Bis dahin hieß sie – nach einem frühen slawischen Fürsten – Budissin. Noch heute wohnt in der Stadt eine sorbische Minderheit mit eigener Sprache und Schulen, an denen die sorbische Sprache gelehrt wird. Bautzen gilt als das politische und kulturelle Zentrum der Sorben in der Oberlausitz.

► Blick auf die Stadtmauer und die Altstadt von Bautzen

► *View to the town wall and the historical town centre of Bautzen*

⌗ *The town of Bautzen is about 30 miles east of Dresden on the banks of the river Spree. The town received its current name only in 1868. Until this date it was named Budissin – after an early Slavic ruler. A Sorbian minority with its own language is still living in the town. Some schools teach their language. Bautzen is the political and cultural capital of the Sorbs.*

▲ Seit 1677 stellen mehr als 120 Werkstätten Meisterinstrumente für Spitzenorchester her.

▲ *Since 1677, more than 120 workshops produce masterpieces for top orchestras.*

Sächsisches Vogtland
Saxon Vogtland

▬ Das Sächsische Vogtland ist der in Sachsen gelegene Teil des Vogtlandes, das sich in Thüringen, Bayern und im tschechischen Böhmen fortsetzt. Die größte Stadt im Sächsischen Vogtland ist Plauen, das durch die Spitzenweberei („Plauener Spitzen") berühmt wurde. Der so genannte Musikwinkel mit Markneukirchen und Klingenthal beliefert heute wie früher die Spitzenorchester in aller Welt mit Meisterinstrumenten.

⌗ *The Saxon Vogtland is a part of the larger region Vogtland, which reaches as far as Bavaria, Thuringia and Bohemia. The largest town of the Saxon Vogtland is Plauen, which became famous for its textile manufacturing capabilities, specialized in lace. The so-called Musikwinkel (music corner) with its towns Markneukirchen and Klingenthal provides musical instruments for top orchestras all over the world.*

Erzgebirge
Ore Mountains

Das Erzgebirge ist ein Mittelgebirge zwischen Sachsen und dem tschechischen Böhmen. Die Kammlagen des bis zu über 1200 m hohen Gebirges sind einem sehr rauen und schneereichen Klima ausgesetzt.

Wie der Name schon andeutet, war das Erzgebirge reich an Erzen. Hier wurden vor allem Silber und Zinn, aber auch Kupfer, Zink und Steinkohle abgebaut. Der Bergbau begann etwa im 14. Jahrhundert und erreichte seinen Höhepunkt im 16. Jahrhundert. Das Silber, das vor Ort zu Silbertalern verarbeitet wurde, begründete den Reichtum Sachsens. Zeitweise wurde mehr Silber gefördert, als Silbergeld geprägt werden konnte.

Heute bietet das Erzgebirge viel für Wanderer und Wintersportler. In der Advents- und Weihnachtszeit ist das Erzgebirge mit seinen Bräuchen, dem traditionellen Weihnachtsschmuck und den bekannten Weihnachtsmärkten ein beliebtes Reiseziel für Kurzurlauber.

The Erzgebirge (Ore Mountains) is a low mountains range between Saxony and Czech Bohemia. The 4,000-foot-high summit area of the mountains is very rough and rich of snow.

As its name says, the Ore Mountains have major deposits of mineral ore. The extraction of silver, tin, copper, zinc and hard coal started in about the 14th century and reached its peak in the 16th century. The silver money made from silver ore on the spot was the basis of the wealth of Saxony. At certain periods, more silver ore was extracted than could be worked.

Today, the Erzgebirge offers a lot for tourists and winter sportsmen. In Advent and during Christmas time, the traditional Christmas fairs with decorations and customs are the reason why the Erzgebirge is a preferred destination for short holidays.

▼ Über 5000 km Wanderwege können im Erzgebirge erkundet werden. Im Winter bieten die Höhenlagen beste Voraussetzungen für den Wintersport.

▼ *More than 3,000 miles of footpaths may be explored in the Ore Mountains. In wintertime, the summit area provides best conditions for winter sports.*

103

Thüringen
Thuringia

▼ Die Gemeinde Mühlberg wurde 704 oder sogar schon früher gegründet.

▼ *The village of Mühlberg was founded in or before 704.*

104

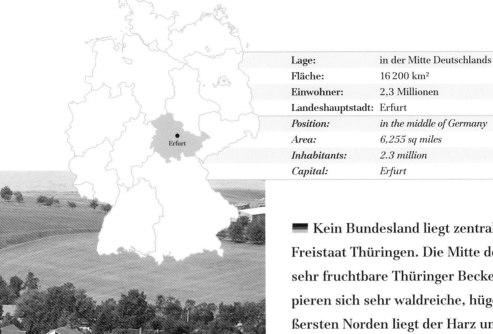

Lage:	in der Mitte Deutschlands
Fläche:	16 200 km²
Einwohner:	2,3 Millionen
Landeshauptstadt:	Erfurt
Position:	*in the middle of Germany*
Area:	*6,255 sq miles*
Inhabitants:	*2.3 million*
Capital:	*Erfurt*

▬ Kein Bundesland liegt zentraler in Deutschland als der Freistaat Thüringen. Die Mitte des Landes nimmt das flache, sehr fruchtbare Thüringer Becken ein. Um diese Region gruppieren sich sehr waldreiche, hügelige Landschaften. Im äußersten Norden liegt der Harz und im Süden erstreckt sich der Thüringer Wald als Mittelgebirge.

Schon sehr frühzeitig war Thüringen ein Königreich, das jedoch im Jahr 531 zerschlagen wurde und dessen Teile unter wechselnder Herrschaft standen. Das heutige Bundesland Thüringen wurde 1990 gegründet.

Thüringen zählt zu den bedeutendsten Kulturregionen in Deutschland. Berühmt sind vor allem die Goethe-Stadt Weimar, die Wartburg und das historische Erfurt.

🇬🇧 *The state of Thuringia is the most central state of Germany. The centre of the state is the very productive flat lowland called Thüringer Becken (Basin). Around this region are a number of densely wooded hilly landscapes. In the very north is the low mountain range Harz and in the south the low mountain range Thuringian Forest.*

In early times, Thuringia was a kingdom which, however, was conquered and divided in 531 and was subject to varying rulers. The current state of Thuringia was founded in 1990.

The land is one of the most important cultural regions in Germany. Especially Goethe's town Weimar, the castle Wartburg and the historical Erfurt are famous.

Erfurt
Erfurt

Landeshauptstadt von Thüringen	
Fläche:	270 km²
Einwohner:	203 000
Capital of Thuringia	
Area:	*104 sq miles*
Inhabitants:	*203,000*

► Eines der Wahrzeichen der Stadt Erfurt ist die Krämerbrücke, die längste bebaute und bewohnte Brücke Europas.

► *One of the symbols of Erfurt is the bridge Krämerbrücke, Europe's largest bridge superstructured with homes.*

◄ Blick über die Stadt Erfurt mit dem Dom St. Marien rechts im Bild

◄ *View over the city of Erfurt with the cathedral St. Marien on the right side*

■ Erfurt wird urkundlich erstmals im Jahr 742 als Bischofssitz erwähnt. Etwa zur selben Zeit wurde auch mit dem Bau des späteren Doms begonnen. Im Jahr 1497 wurde die Hauptglocke des Doms, die so genannte Maria Gloriosa, gegossen, die heute noch zu besonderen Ereignissen und kirchlichen Feiertagen geläutet wird. Die Gloriosa wiegt 11,4 Tonnen, hat einen Durchmesser von 2,56 m und ist die größte mittelalterliche Glocke der Welt.

Die 1392 gegründete Universität Erfurt war zeitweise die größte Universität des Landes. Ihr berühmtester Student ist Martin Luther, der an der philosophischen Fakultät von Erfurt die Magister-Prüfung ablegte.

Der noch sehr junge „Thüringer Zoopark Erfurt" im Norden der Stadt gehört zu den flächenmäßig größten Zoos in Deutschland. Das Aquarium besitzt eine der größten Sammlungen an Süßwasserfischen in Deutschland.

🇬🇧 *The oldest historical records about Erfurt – as a bishopric – are from 742. About the same time the construction of the later cathedral started. The main bell of the cathedral, the so-called Maria Gloriosa, was cast in 1497 and is still being operated at special events and church ceremonies. The Gloriosa is the largest medieval bell n the world, is 11.4 metric tons in weight and 8.4 feet in diameter.*

The University of Erfurt which was established in 1392 was for a certain period the largest one of the country. Its most famous student is Martin Luther who received his master's degree at the philosophic faculty.

The very young Thuringian Zoo Park in the north of the city is in terms of square miles one of the largest zoos in Germany. The aquarium has one of the most significant collections of freshwater fishes.

▼ Schloss Friedenstein war eine Residenz der Herzöge von Sachsen-Gotha.

▼ *The palace Friedenstein was the residence of the dukes of Saxe-Gotha.*

Gotha
Gotha

■ Etwa 20 km westlich von Erfurt liegt die Stadt Gotha, die von 1640 bis 1920 Hauptstadt des Herzogtums Sachsen-Gotha war. Ein Sitz der Adligen war das Schloss Friedenstein. Das Schloss besitzt den ältesten Englischen Garten auf dem Festland und das älteste noch erhaltene Schlosstheater der Welt mit der originalen Bühnenmechanik aus dem Barock. In Gotha wurde im Jahr 1820 mit der „Gothaer Feuerversicherungsbank" das deutsche Versicherungswesen begründet. Bekannt ist auch „Der Gotha", der Gothaische Genealogische Hofkalender, dessen erster Vorgänger 1763 erschien.

🇬🇧 *About 12 miles west of Erfurt is the town of Gotha, which was the capital of the duchy of Saxe-Gotha from 1640 to 1920. The palace Schloss Friedenstein was a ducal residence. It has the oldest English style garden on the European continent and has the oldest preserved palace theatre of the world with an original Baroque stage technique. It was in 1820 in Gotha, when the German insurance system was founded. The Almanach de Gotha, published from 1763, was a respected directory of Europe's highest nobility and royalty.*

Im äußersten Westen Thüringens – etwa 50 km westlich von Erfurt – liegt die Stadt Eisenach. Die über der Stadt gelegene Wartburg war im Mittelalter Sitz der Landgrafen von Thüringen. Bekannt wurden Eisenach und die Wartburg durch Martin Luther, der hier das Neue Testament vom Griechischen ins Deutsche übersetzte. Die Burg mit der „Lutherstube" gehört zum UNESCO-Weltkulturerbe und ist ein bedeutendes Ziel des kulturell orientierten Tourismus. Eisenach ist auch die Geburtsstadt des Komponisten und damals schon berühmten Organisten Johann Sebastian Bach.

Die in der zweiten Hälfte des 19. Jahrhunderts einsetzende Industrialisierung machte Eisenach zum heute größten Industriezentrum Thüringens. Im Jahr 1896 wurde das Automobilwerk Eisenach gegründet, das vorübergehend zu den Bayerischen Motorenwerken gehörte und das später die DDR-Limousine „Wartburg" baute. Auch nach der Wiedervereinigung wurde die Tradition des Automobilbaus fortgesetzt.

▼ Die Wartburg, auf der Martin Luther das Neue Testament aus dem Griechischen ins Deutsche übersetzte, gehört seit 1999 zum UNESCO-Weltkulturerbe.

▼ *The castle Wartburg where Martin Luther translated the New Testament from Greek into German has been a cultural world heritage site since 1999.*

The town of Eisenach is in the very west of Thuringia – about 30 miles west of Erfurt. The castle Wartburg above the town was the medieval residence of the landgraves of Thuringia. The castle as well as the town became famous by Martin Luther, who translated the New Testament from Greek into German. The Wartburg with Luther's room "Lutherstube" is a cultural world heritage site and is an important destination for culturally oriented tourists. Also, Eisenach is the birth town of the composer and – already in his time famous – organist Johann Sebastian Bach.

During the second half of the 19th century Eisenach developed into the largest industrial centre of Thuringia. In 1896 the motorcar factory Eisenach was established, which for a short period belonged to the Bavaria Motor Company (BMW) and which later on produced the GDR top limousine "Wartburg". After the reunification of Germany, Eisenach continued the tradition of car manufacturing, too.

Arnstadt
Arnstadt

▬ Etwa 20 km südlich von Erfurt liegt die ehemalige Residenzstadt der Grafen von Schwarzburg. Deren Residenz, Schloss Neideck, wurde um die Mitte des 16. Jahrhunderts erbaut. Im Jahr
1703 fand der 18-jährige Johann Sebastian Bach in Arnstadt eine
Anstellung als Organist der Neuen Kirche. Vier Jahre später ver-
ließ er wieder die Stadt, nachdem er Meinungsverschiedenheiten
mit dem Stadtrat hatte.

🇬🇧 *About 12 miles south of Erfurt is the former residence town of
the counts of Schwarzburg. Their palace Schloss Neideck was built
in the middle of the 16th century. In 1703, the 18-year-old Johann
Sebastian Bach was engaged as organist of the church Neue Kirche
at Arnstadt. Four years later, he left the town after having had
some trouble with the town council.*

◄ Denkmal des jungen Organisten
Johann Sebastian Bach in Arnstadt

◄ *Monument to the young organist
Johann Sebastian Bach at Arnstadt*

Meiningen
Meiningen

▬ Im Südwesten Thüringens,
an der Werra, bildet die Stadt
Meiningen den Schnittpunkt
zweier mittelalterlicher Handelsstraßen. Durch Leinenweberei
und Stoffhandel gelangte Meiningen zu Wohlstand und wurde
Residenzstadt des Herzogtums
Sachsen-Meiningen. Die 1690
gegründete Hofkapelle ist eine
der traditionsreichsten in
Europa. Hofkapellmeister waren
hier unter anderem Richard
Strauss und Max Reger.

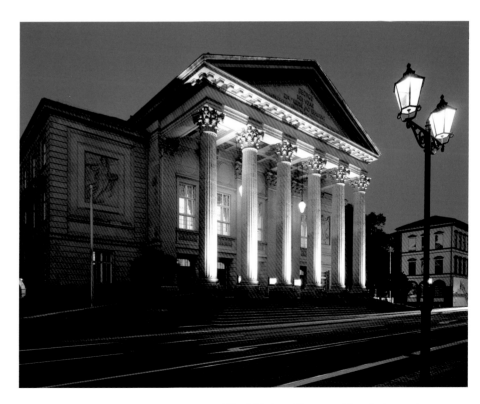

🇬🇧 *In the south-west of Thuringia, on the banks of the river Werra,
the town of Meiningen is at the intersection of two medieval trading
routes. The town prospered by linen weaving as well as textile trading and became the residence town of the dukes of Saxe-Meiningen.
The court orchestra founded in 1690 is one of the richest in tradition
with men like Richard Strauss and Max Reger as directors of music.*

▲ Das Meininger Theater gehörte in der zweiten Hälfte des 19. Jahrhunderts zur europäischen Spitze.

▲ *During the second half of the 19th century,
the theatre of Meiningen was one of the top
theatres in Europe.*

Die 20 km östlich von Erfurt gelegene Stadt Weimar ist einer der bedeutsamsten Orte in Deutschland. Der Herzog von Sachsen-Weimar-Eisenach holte Johann Wolfgang Goethe nach Weimar und übertrug ihm hohe Regierungsämter. Ebenso wurden die Dichter Schiller, Herder und Wieland sowie die Komponisten Franz Liszt und Richard Wagner nach Weimar geholt. Wagners Oper Lohengrin wurde in Weimar uraufgeführt.

Im Jahr 1919 wurde im Deutschen Nationaltheater in Weimar die erste republikanische Verfassung für Deutschland beschlossen. Die Ära von 1919 bis 1933 ist bekannt als „Weimarer Republik".

The town of Weimar 12 miles east of Erfurt is one of the most significant towns in Germany. The Duke of Saxe-Weimar-Eisenach brought Johann Wolfgang Goethe to Weimar and gave him high governmental positions. In a similar way the poets Schiller, Herder and Wieland as well as the composers Franz Liszt and Richard Wagner were transferred to Weimar. Wagner's opera Lohengrin was first performed in Weimar.

In 1919, the first democratic constitution for Germany was passed by the National Congress. The time from 1919 to 1933 is known as "Weimar Republic".

❚ Das barocke Schloss Belvedere südlich von Weimar wurde 1724 bis 1732 als herzögliche Residenz erbaut.

❚ *The baroque palace Belvedere south of Weimar was constructed from 1724 to 1732 as a ducal residence.*

110

🇩🇪 Gera ist die zweitgrößte Stadt Thüringens und liegt im Osten des Bundeslandes. Seit 1564 war Gera Residenzstadt des Fürstenhauses Reuß und kam durch seine Textilwirtschaft zu erheblichem Wohlstand. Im 19. Jahrhundert entwickelte sich Gera zu einem Industriezentrum. Während der DDR-Zeit war der Uranabbau im angrenzenden Ronneburg der wichtigste Wirtschaftszweig für Gera und die Region. Zeitweise wurden hier 11 Prozent des weltweit abgebauten Urans gefördert.

🇬🇧 *Gera is the second largest town in Thuringia and is located in the east of the state. Since 1564, Gera was the residence town of the royal house Reuß and prospered very well thanks to its textile manufacturing. In the 19th century, Gera developed into an industrial centre. Under the rule of the GDR, the exploitation of uranium deposits in the neighbouring town Ronneburg was the most important economic branch of the region. At times, 11 percent of the world's uranium production came from here.*

▴ Goethe und Schiller – das wohl bekannteste Denkmal in Deutschland

▴ *Goethe and Schiller – probably the most famous monument in Germany*

▾ Das Rathaus von Gera, das 1576 vollendet wurde, gehört zu den bedeutenden touristischen Anziehungspunkten.

▾ *The historical town hall of Gera, finished in 1576, is a significant tourist attraction.*

111

Im östlichen Teil Thüringens – im Tal der Saale – liegt die Universitätsstadt Jena. Zu Beginn des 18. Jahrhunderts nahm Jena bei der Studentenzahl eine Spitzenstellung ein. 1846 gründete Carl Zeiss in Jena eine optische Werkstätte, die er zusammen mit Ernst Abbe zu einer weltweit bekannten Firma für Mikroskope und andere optische Geräte aufbaute. Aus einem gemeinsamen „Glastechnischen Laboratorium" von Otto Schott, Ernst Abbe und Carl Zeiss ging eine der bedeutendsten Glasfabriken hervor. „Jenaer Glas" wurde zum Inbegriff für feuerfestes Glas.

Die optische Industrie in Jena zählt heute nach Jahren des Wiederaufbaus wieder zur technologischen Weltspitze. Das Schott-Glas-Museum bietet Einblicke in die Produktion und Verwendung von Glas. Im Optischen Museum findet man eine Ausstellung zur Geschichte optischer Geräte wie Brillen oder Mikroskope. Mit dem 159 m hohen so genannten JenTower besitzt Jena das höchste Bürogebäude der neuen Bundesländer.

In the eastern part of Thuringia, in the valley of the river Saale, is the university city of Jena. At the beginning of the 18th century, Jena had a top number of students. In 1846, Carl Zeiss founded in Jena a workshop for optical instruments, which expanded into a world famous factory for microscopes and optical systems. A "Glass Laboratory" run by Otto Schott, Ernst Abbe and Carl Zeiss was the germ cell of one of the most important glass production facilities. "Jena Glass" became the synonym of fire resistant types of glass.

Now, after years of reconstruction, the optical industry of Jena is again among the world's leaders in technology. The Schott Glass Museum gives an insight into the production and application of glass. The Optical Museum presents an exhibition about the history of optical instruments like glasses or microscopes. The 522-foot-high JenTower is the highest office building of the "new" Federal States.

❚ Blick über Jena mit dem 1972 erbauten JenTower, der zu einem Wahrzeichen Thüringens wurde

❚ *View over Jena with its so-called JenTower from 1972 which became a symbol of Thuringia*

► Im Jahr 1865 inspirierte das enge und felsige Trusetal die Leute, den Fluss umzuleiten und ein Naturdenkmal zu schaffen – den Wasserfall.

► In 1865, the narrow and rocky valley of the river Truse inspired men to divert the river in order to create a natural monument – the water falls.

Thüringer Wald
Thuringian Forest

■ Südlich von Erfurt verläuft der Thüringer Wald auf etwa 150 km Länge von Nordwesten nach Südosten. Er ist ein sehr waldreiches Mittelgebirge. Das im östlichen Bereich angrenzende Thüringer Schiefergebirge wird im Allgemeinen dem Thüringer Wald hinzugerechnet. Die höchsten Berge sind knapp 1000 m hoch. In Kammnähe verläuft die Wasserscheide zwischen Elbe im Norden und Werra–Weser bzw. Main–Rhein im Süden.

Fast genau in der Mitte des Thüringer Walds liegt Suhl, die größte Stadt der Region. Im frühen 16. Jahrhundert ließen sich Nürnberger und Augsburger Büchsenschmiede in Suhl nieder und begründeten eine bis heute andauernde Tradition. Sport- und Jagdwaffen aus Suhl sind weltberühmt.

Auf dem Kamm des Thüringer Waldes verläuft von Eisenach bis nach Blankenstein an der Saale der 168 km lange „Rennsteig", einer der beliebtesten Höhenwanderwege in Deutschland. Im Jahr 2000 wurde auch ein Rennsteig-Radwanderweg eröffnet, der zwar 30 km länger ist als der Fußwanderweg, aber starke Steigungen vermeidet. Entlang des Rennsteigs gibt es zahlreiche Übernachtungsmöglichkeiten.

113

▧ *South of Erfurt, the 90-miles Thuringian Forest runs from the north-west to the south-east. It is a densely wooded low mountain range. The neighbouring area Thüringer Schiefergebirge is usually regarded as a part of the Thuringian Forest. The altitude of the summits is close to 3,300 feet. Along the summits runs the watershed between the river Elbe in the north and the rivers Werra–Weser and Main–Rhine in the south.*

Almost in the middle of the Thuringian Forest is the largest town of the region, Suhl. In the early 16th century, gunsmiths from Nuremberg and Augsburg settled in Suhl and started a tradition still living today. Sporting and hunting weapons from Suhl are famous all over the world.

Along the crest – from Eisenach to Blankenstein on the banks of the river Saale – runs one of Germany's most popular hiking routes, the 100-mile so-called Rennsteig. In 2000, an additional bicycle route was opened which is 20 miles longer but less steep than the hiking route. Along the routes there is overnight accommodation at many places.

Hessen
Hesse

▼ Die Skyline von Frankfurt wird manchmal auch „Mainhattan" genannt.

▼ *The Skyline of Frankfurt is sometimes called "Mainhattan".*

114

Lage:	in der westlichen Mitte Deutschlands
Fläche:	21 100 km²
Einwohner:	6,1 Millionen
Landeshauptstadt:	Wiesbaden
Position:	*in the western middle of Germany*
Area:	*8,150 sq miles*
Inhabitants:	*6.1 million*
Capital:	*Wiesbaden*

▬ Das Land Hessen liegt in der Mitte Deutschlands und grenzt an sechs andere Bundesländer. Es wurde in seiner heutigen Form 1945 aus den Territorien mehrerer Fürstentümer gegründet. Hessens Landschaft besteht aus zahlreichen Mittelgebirgen – darunter der Taunus, der Odenwald und der Westerwald – und einigen Niederungen im Rhein-Main-Gebiet und in der Wetterau.

Im südlichen Hessen ist das Rhein-Main-Gebiet um Frankfurt, Wiesbaden und Darmstadt ein wirtschaftlich außerordentlich starker, dicht besiedelter Ballungsraum mit vielen Industrie- und Dienstleistungsunternehmen. Dagegen ist der nördliche Teil Hessens mit seiner historischen Hauptstadt Kassel eher ländlich geprägt.

🇬🇧 *The state of Hesse is in the middle of Germany and has six other states as neighbours. Hesse was founded in 1945 and configured from the territory of several principalities. The Hesse landscape has numerous low mountain areas – such as Taunus, Odenwald and Westerwald – and some flat lowlands in the Rhine-Main region and Wetterau.*

In southern Hesse, the Rhine-Main region around the cities Frankfurt, Wiesbaden and Darmstadt is an economically powerful and densely populated conurbation with many industry and service enterprises. In contrast to the south, the northern part of Hesse with its historical capital Kassel is more rural.

Wiesbaden
Wiesbaden

Landeshauptstadt von Hessen	
Fläche:	204 km²
Einwohner:	276 000
Capital of Hesse	
Area:	*80 sq miles*
Inhabitants:	*276,000*

► Das heutige Kurhaus wurde von Kaiser Wilhelm II. in Auftrag gegeben und ersetzte ein Gebäude aus dem Jahr 1810.

► *The present-day health centre of Wiesbaden was commissioned by Emperor Wilhelm II and replaced a building from 1810.*

◄ Das Kurhaus, in dem sich die Wiesbadener Spielbank befindet, wurde 1907 eröffnet und 1985 aufwändig restauriert.

◄ *The health resort, in which the casino of Wiesbaden is located, was opened in 1907 and lavishly restored in 1985.*

▬ Die Landeshauptstadt Wiesbaden ist mit ihren 26 Thermalquellen eines der ältesten Kurbäder Europas. Schon die Römer wussten die heißen Quellen zu schätzen und errichteten hier kurz nach der Zeitenwende ein befestigtes Lager.

Die vielleicht glanzvollste Zeit erlebte Wiesbaden als „Kaiserstadt" im späten 19. Jahrhundert, als sich der kaiserliche Hofstaat zur Sommerfrische hier niederließ und zahlreiche Adlige, Künstler und reiche Bürger folgten. Aus dieser Epoche stammen die großzügigen und repräsentativen Gebäude in der weitgehend unversehrt gebliebenen Innenstadt.

Den Mittelpunkt der historischen Altstadt bildet der Schlossplatz, auf dem unter anderem das 1610 erbaute Alte Rathaus steht. Das gegenüberliegende Stadtschloss der Herzöge von Nassau nutzte Kaiser Wilhelm II. während seiner Aufenthalte in Wiesbaden. Heute residiert hier der Hessische Landtag.

⬛ *The capital Wiesbaden with its 26 thermal springs is one of the oldest spas in Europe. Already the Romans enjoyed the hot springs and founded a fortress 2,000 years ago.*

Probably the most splendid time was in the late 19th century when the imperial household came to Wiesbaden for summer holidays, followed by numerous aristocrats, artists and rich people. The spacious and representative buildings of the well preserved city centre are from these times.

The focal point of the historical town centre is the square Schlossplatz with the old town hall Altes Rathaus from 1610. On the opposite side of the square, the city palace of the Dukes of Nassau was utilized by Emperor Wilhelm II during his stays in Wiesbaden. Today, the Stadtschloss serves as the residence of the Hessian parliament.

▼ Die Russische Kapelle, die für Zar Nikolaus II. gebaut wurde, der oft Darmstadt besuchte

▼ *The Russian Chapel which was constructed for Tsar Nikolaus II who frequently stayed at Darmstadt*

Darmstadt
Darmstadt

▬ Weit im Süden Hessens liegt Darmstadt. Aus einer mittelalterlichen Siedlung der Franken heraus entwickelte sich nach einer wechselvollen Geschichte eine moderne Industrie- und Universitätsstadt mit rund 30 000 Studenten. Im Gefolge der technisch orientierten Universität haben sich in Darmstadt zahlreiche Forschungsinstitute und Unternehmen der Informations- und Kommunikationstechnologie angesiedelt. Ein gebürtiger Darmstädter ist der berühmte Chemiker Justus von Liebig, der unter anderem das Backpulver erfand.

⬛ *The city of Darmstadt is in the very south of Hesse. From a medieval Franconian settlement and after a varied history, the town developed into a modern industrial city. Its university has about 30,000 students. In the wake of the technical oriented university numerous research institutes and companies settled there, which work in the field of information and communication technologies. The famous chemist Justus von Liebig, inventor of baking powder, was born in Darmstadt.*

Rüdesheim
Rüdesheim

Westlich von Wiesbaden liegt am nördlichen Rheinufer die kleine Winzerstadt Rüdesheim. Spätestens seit dem Mittelalter, vermutlich aber schon seit der Römerzeit vor 2000 Jahren, wird an den steilen Südhängen Weinbau betrieben. Der mittelalterliche Ortskern und die Lage im Rheingau, einem der weltweit besten Weinanbaugebiete, haben Rüdesheim zu einer der größten Touristen-Attraktionen in Deutschland gemacht.

West of Wiesbaden on the northern banks of the river Rhine is the little wine growing town Rüdesheim. At the latest from the Middle Ages, more probably from the times of the Romans, wine has been cultivated on the steep southern slopes. The medieval centre of the town as well as its location in the Rheingau region, which is one of the worldwide best wine-growing areas, has made Rüdesheim one of the most attractive tourist destinations in Germany.

▲ Eine Seilbahn führt hinauf zum Niederwalddenkmal mit der „Germania".

▲ *A cable car takes the tourists up to the "Germania" monument.*

Wetzlar
Wetzlar

Am nördlichen Rand des Naturparks Hochtaunus liegt auf einem Hügel die Stadt Wetzlar. Die historische Altstadt mit ihren Fachwerkhäusern wurde weitgehend zur Fußgängerzone erklärt. Am Fuße der Altstadt führt eine 750 Jahre alte Brücke über die Lahn. Nichtsdestoweniger ist Wetzlar eine bedeutende Industriestadt. Die von Ernst Leitz gegründete Firma für optische Geräte genoss bereits vor 100 Jahren Weltruf.

The town of Wetzlar is on a hill of the northern edge of the natural park Hochtaunus. The old historical centre with its half-timbered houses is to its major part a pedestrian area. At the foot of the old town, a 750-year-old bridge leads across the river Lahn. Nevertheless, Wetzlar is an important industrial town. Ernst Leitz founded a production facility for optical instruments there, which gained world fame already 100 years ago.

◄ Wetzlar mit der alten Brücke und dem Dom, dessen Grundstein 1230 gelegt wurde, der aber mehrmals im Mittelalter umgebaut wurde

◄ *Wetzlar with the old bridge and the cathedral which was founded in 1230 but was altered many times in the Middle Ages*

Frankfurt
Frankfurt

Frankfurt am Main ist mit über 660 000 Einwohnern die größte Stadt Hessens. In der Gesamtregion Frankfurt wohnen rund 5 Millionen Menschen. Seit dem Mittelalter gehört Frankfurt zu den bedeutendsten Zentren in Deutschland.

Das Wahrzeichen der Stadt ist der „Römer", ein Ensemble aus drei ursprünglich eigenständigen Häusern. Der Römer ist seit 600 Jahren das Rathaus der Stadt Frankfurt und gleichzeitig der Ort, an dem die meisten Könige und Kaiser gewählt und gekrönt wurden. 1749 wurde in Frankfurt der Dichter Johann Wolfgang Goethe geboren.

Das heutige Stadtbild wird durch die modernen Hochhäuser im „Bankenviertel" geprägt. Frankfurt ist Sitz der Europäischen Zentralbank und neben London der wichtigste Finanzplatz Europas. Die seit dem 15. Jahrhundert stattfindende Frankfurter Buchmesse ist nicht nur die größte Buchmesse der Welt, sondern auch ein herausragendes kulturelles Ereignis.

Frankfurt am Main has more than 660,000 inhabitants and is the largest city of Hesse. Greater Frankfurt has about 5 million inhabitants. Since the Middle Ages, Frankfurt has been one of the most important centres in Germany.

The symbol of the city, the so-called Römer, is an ensemble of three originally independent buildings. Since 600 years, the Römer has served as town hall of Frankfurt. It is also the place where most of the kings and emperors have been elected and crowned. In 1749, the poet Johann Wolfgang Goethe was born in Frankfurt.

The today's face of the city is characterized by modern skyscrapers in the "banking quarter". Frankfurt is the residence of the European Central Bank and is, beside London, the most important financial market place in Europe. The Frankfurt Book Fair is not only the world's largest book fair but also an extraordinary cultural event.

❚ Die Alte Oper in Frankfurt, die 1944 völlig zerstört, originalgetreu wiederaufgebaut und 1981 wiedereröffnet wurde

❚ *The so-called Old Opera House in Frankfurt which was destroyed in 1944, rebuilt, true to the original, and reopened in 1981*

119

Marburg
Marburg

▬ Etwa 80 km nördlich von Frankfurt liegt am Ufer der Lahn die Universitätsstadt Marburg. Die Stadt entstand unterhalb einer Burg, die vermutlich im 9. Jahrhundert erbaut wurde. Im Jahr 1228 ließ sich die später heilig gesprochene Elisabeth von Thüringen in Marburg nieder, wo sie ein Hospital baute und sich der Krankenpflege widmete.

1527 – während der Reformationszeit – gründete Philipp der Großmütige in Marburg die erste protestantische Universität, die seitdem die Stadt Marburg entscheidend geprägt hat. Ein berühmt gewordener Marburger Student war der russische Dichter Boris Pasternak, der 1958 den Nobelpreis für Literatur erhielt. Der Chirurg Professor Ferdinand Sauerbruch begann seine Karriere als Oberarzt an der Universität Marburg.

Marburg liegt zum Teil an den Hängen des relativ engen Tals der Lahn. Einige Stadtteile sind durch öffentliche Aufzüge miteinander verbunden.

⌗ *About 50 miles north of Frankfurt, on the banks of the river Lahn, is the town of Marburg. The town is overlooked by a castle which was probably built in the 9th century. In 1228 Elisabeth of Thuringia, who was later canonized, settled in Marburg, where she built a hospital and devoted her life to the poor.*

In 1527, Philip the Magnanimous established the first Protestant university, which significantly characterized the town of Marburg. A Marburg student who became famous was the Russian poet Boris Pasternak, who received the Nobel Prize for Literature in 1958. The surgeon Ferdinand Sauerbruch started his career at the University of Marburg. The town is partly on the hills of the relatively narrow valley of the river Lahn. Some parts of the town are connected with each other via public elevators.

◄ Die Altstadt von Marburg hat nach Jacob Grimm „mehr Treppen auf der Straße als in den Häusern."

◄ *The historical town centre of Marburg is said to have more flights of steps in its streets than staircases in its homes.*

Gießen
Gießen

▬ Fast im Zentrum Hessens liegt die Universitätsstadt Gießen. Sie entstand als Siedlung in unmittelbarer Nähe einer im Jahr 1152 gegründeten Burg. Das Recht zur Errichtung einer Universität erhielt die Stadt im Jahr 1607. Der vielleicht bekannteste Professor an der Universität Gießen war Wilhelm Conrad Röntgen, der für die Entdeckung der nach ihm benannten Strahlen den ersten Nobelpreis für Physik (1901) erhielt.

▲ Das Stadttheater von Gießen

▲ *The municipal theatre of the town of Gießen*

🇬🇧 *Almost in the middle of Hesse is the university town of Gießen, which developed from a settlement near a castle, which was founded in 1152. In 1607, the town received the right to found a university. Probably the best known professor at the University of Gießen was Wilhelm Conrad Röntgen, who discovered X-rays and received the Nobel Prize for Physics in 1901.*

Bad Hersfeld
Bad Hersfeld

▬ Im Nordosten von Hessen liegt die Kurstadt Bad Hersfeld, deren Gründung auf eine Abtei aus dem 8. Jahrhundert zurückgeht. Deren erster Abt hieß Lullus und nach ihm ist die Heilquelle benannt, deren Wasser aus 422 m Tiefe kommt. Die eisen- und bittersalzhaltige Quelle war bereits im 16. Jahrhundert bekannt und wird heute bei Erkrankungen des Magens und des Darmes angewendet.

🇬🇧 *In the north-east of Hesse is the spa Bad Hersfeld, which was founded from a monastery in the 8th century. The first abbot's name was Lullus. After him the medicinal spring is named, from which the water comes from 1,400 feet in depth. The spring, which contains iron as well as Epsom salts, was already known in the 16th century and is today used in case of stomach or intestinal troubles.*

► Bad Hersfeld ist bekannt für die Freilichtaufführungen in der Stiftsruine, einer der größten Kirchenruinen.

► *Bad Hersfeld is well known for its open air theatre located in one of the largest church ruins.*

Odenwald
Odenwald

Im äußersten Süden des Landes liegt der Odenwald, der im Westen an die Oberrheinische Tiefebene angrenzt und sich im Süden bis nach Baden erstreckt. In vorchristlicher Zeit war die von Urwald bedeckte Region von Kelten und später von Germanen besiedelt. Nach einer teilweisen Besetzung durch die Römer folgten Alemannen und dann Franken. Der Nibelungensage nach wurde der Drachentöter Siegfried bei der Jagd im Odenwald – an der so genannten Siegfriedstraße – ermordet.

Im Norden des Odenwalds ist die Feste Breuberg eine der besterhaltenen Burgen Deutschlands. Im Süden, bereits auf badischem Gebiet, steht die Burg Guttenberg aus dem 12. Jahrhundert, die – nahezu einmalig – seit dem Mittelalter nie zerstört wurde und noch immer bewohnt ist.

Eine Sehenswürdigkeit im Zentrum des Odenwalds ist das Rathaus von Michelstadt, das 1484 erbaut wurde. Das Fachwerkhaus ruht auf Eichenstelzen und stellt dadurch eine teilweise Überdachung des Marktplatzes dar.

In the very south of the state is the Odenwald region, which in the south reaches into the state of Baden-Wurttemberg. In former times, the region was covered with primeval forest and was first settled by Celts, then by German tribes and then partly by the Romans who were followed by Alemanns and Franks. According to the legend of the Nibelungs, the hunting dragon-slayer Siegfried was murdered in the Odenwald not far from the so-called Siegfried route.

In the north of the Odenwald is the fortress Breuberg, which is one of the best preserved castles in Germany. In the south, already in the region of Baden, is the 12th century castle of Guttenberg, which had never been damaged since the Middle Ages and which is still in use as a home.

Worth seeing in the central Odenwald is the town hall of Michelstadt, which was built in 1484. The half-timbered house stands on oak stilts and serves as a cover for the market place.

▼ Burg und Stadt Hirschhorn werden auch „Perle des Neckartals" genannt.

▼ *The castle and town of Hirschhorn are called "pearl of the Neckar valley".*

▲ Die Taunusbahn bei Neu-Anspach
führt an blühenden Rapsfeldern vorbei.
Im Hintergrund der Große Feldberg.

▲ *The Taunus Railway passing blooming
rape fields near the town of Neu-Anspach. In the background is the mountain
Großer Feldberg.*

Taunus
Taunus

▬ Der Taunus ist ein Mittelgebirge nördlich
von Wiesbaden. Die westliche Grenze bildet
der Rhein. Im Osten reicht der Taunus bis an
die Wetterau, die Ebene nördlich von Frankfurt. Die klimatisch günstig gelegenen Süd-
hänge im Bereich des Rheins genießen als
Weinbaugebiet „Rheingau" Weltruf.

Der Taunus ist reich an Mineral- und Heilquel-
len, die zum Teil schon von den Römern genutzt wurden. Etwa ab dem 17. Jahrhundert
entstanden zahlreiche Heilbäder, zum Beispiel
Bad Soden oder später Bad Homburg. Die Mi-
neralquellen in Oberselters, einem Stadtteil
von Bad Camberg, sind zum Synonym für Mi-
neralwasser („Selters") geworden.

Im Taunus liegen insgesamt drei Naturparks,
die von einem großen Netz an Wanderwegen,
darunter zwei Europäischen Fernwanderwe-
gen, erschlossen werden. Die höchste Erhebung im Taunus ist der 980 m hohe Große
Feldberg, von dessen Aussichtsturm man bis
nach Frankfurt sehen kann.

⚓ *The Taunus is a low mountain range north of Wiesbaden. Its western edge runs along the river Rhine. In the east, the Taunus runs into
the Wetterau region, which is the lowland north of Frankfurt. The southern slopes close to the Rhine enjoy a favourable climate and have, as the
wine-growing area Rheingau, worldwide reputation.*

*The Taunus is rich in mineral springs, which were used already by the
Romans. From the 17th century, numerous spas were founded, such as
Bad Soden or later on Bad Homburg. The mineral springs of Oberselters, which is a district of the town of Bad Camberg, became a synonym
for soda water ("Selters").*

*Within the Taunus are three natural parks, which are opened up by
a network of hiking routes, among them two European long-distance
paths. The top peak of the Taunus is the 3,215-feet Großer Feldberg,
of which the observation tower allows one to see as far as Frankfurt.*

Lahn
River Lahn

■ Die Lahn entspringt in Nordrhein-Westfalen und fließt zunächst nach Osten auf hessisches Gebiet, dann in Richtung Süden durch Marburg und Gießen und schließlich nach Westen über Wetzlar, Limburg und Bad Ems, um bei Koblenz in den Rhein zu münden. Die Lahn, die von der Mündung bis nach Wetzlar mit kleinen Motorbooten befahren werden kann, ist wegen ihres naturnahen Verlaufs bei Wassersportlern sehr beliebt.

The river Lahn rises in North-Rhine Westphalia and first runs towards the east into Hesse, then towards the south via Marburg and Gießen and finally towards the west via Wetzlar, Limburg and Bad Ems. Near Koblenz, the Lahn joins the river Rhine. From its mouth up to Wetzlar, the river Lahn is navigable for smaller motor boats. Because of its natural course the river is a very popular water sports area.

▲ Limburg an der Lahn mit dem St.-Georg-Dom

▲ *The river Lahn passing Limburg cathedral St. Georg*

Main
River Main

■ Der Main ist der längste rechte Nebenfluss des Rheins. In vielen großen Windungen kommt er aus dem bayerischen Franken, erreicht hinter Aschaffenburg hessisches Gebiet und mündet bei Wiesbaden in den Rhein. Er ist eine wichtige Wasserstraße. Vor allem im Ballungsraum um Frankfurt befinden sich mehrere große Binnenhäfen. Über den Main-Donau-Kanal ist der Main mit der Donau und letztlich mit dem Schwarzen Meer verbunden.

The river Main is the longest tributary right of the Rhine. Coming from Bavaria in many large meanders, the river reaches the state of Hesse just beyond Aschaffenburg. Not far from Wiesbaden the Main joins the river Rhine. The Main is an important water way. Within the conurbation area around Frankfurt are several large river ports. Via the Main-Danube-Canal the Main is connected to the Black Sea.

◄ Das Mainufer mit der Frankfurter Skyline im Hintergrund ist ein Anziehungspunkt für Spaziergänger.

◄ *The banks of the river Main with the Frankfurt skyline in the background are an attractive goal for walkers.*

Kassel
Kassel

Die Stadt Kassel liegt im Norden von Hessen nahe der Grenze zu Niedersachsen. Die Gründung der Stadt geht auf einen Königshof aus dem 10. Jahrhundert zurück. Im 13. Jahrhundert wurde Kassel zur Hauptstadt der Landgrafschaft bzw. ab 1803 des Kurfürstentums Hessen. Mit der Besetzung des Kurfürstentums durch Preußen im Jahr 1866 endet die Rolle Kassels als Haupt- und Residenzstadt.

Unter den Landgrafen und Kurfürsten von Hessen als Bauherren wurde im Stadtgebiet von Kassel der barocke Bergpark Wilhelmshöhe angelegt. Er ist der größte Bergpark in Europa und mit seinen Kasseler Wasserspielen ein Landschaftspark von Weltgeltung. Die heutige Form des Bergparks Wilhelmshöhe ist kein ausschließlicher Barockgarten, sondern teilweise eher ein Englischer Landschaftspark.

International bekannt ist Kassel auch durch die seit 1955 alle vier bis fünf Jahre stattfindende Kunstausstellung „documenta".

The city of Kassel is in the north of Hesse close to Lower Saxony. The founding of the town dates back to a royal court from the 10th century. In the 13th century, Kassel became the capital of the earldom and from 1803 capital of the electorate Hesse. In 1866, when Prussia occupied the electorate, Kassel's role as a capital and residence town came to an end.

Under the rule of the landgraves and electors, the Baroque mountain park Wilhemshöhe – just within the town area – was created. It is the largest mountain park in Europe and, with its long sets of artificial cascades, worth seeing. The present-day appearance of the park Wilhelmshöhe is not exclusively Baroque but partly an English style landscape garden.

Kassel is internationally famous for its shows of contemporary art, "documenta", which have been held every four to five years since 1955.

▼ Der Apollotempel im Bergpark Wilhelmshöhe wurde nach dem römischen Gott der Weisheit benannt. Er wird aber auch Tempel der Freundschaft genannt.

▼ *The Apollo Temple in the mountain park Wilhelmshöhe is called after the Roman god of wisdom. However, it is also called Temple of Friendship.*

Rheinland-Pfalz
Rhineland-Palatinate

Das Rheintal mit dem Loreley-Felsen bei
Sankt Goarshausen

The Rhine valley with the Loreley-Rocks
near Sankt Goarshausen

126

Lage:	im Südwesten Deutschlands
Fläche:	19 800 km²
Einwohner:	6,1 Millionen
Landeshauptstadt:	Mainz
Position:	*in the south-west of Germany*
Area:	*7,660 sq miles*
Inhabitants:	*6.1 million*
Capital:	*Mainz*

▬ Das Land Rheinland-Pfalz liegt im Südwesten Deutschlands und grenzt an Frankreich, Belgien und Luxemburg. Das Land wurde 1946 aus bayerischen, hessischen und preußischen „Provinzen" und Regierungsbezirken gebildet.

Auf dem Gebiet des heutigen Bundeslandes hatte schon der römische Feldherr Julius Cäsar Brücken über den Rhein gebaut. Aus der Zeit der Römer stammen auch verschiedene Städte, zum Beispiel Mainz, Koblenz und Trier. Im Mittelalter wurden zahllose Burgen an und über den Flüssen Rhein und Mosel gebaut.

Das Bundesland erbringt eine hohe Wirtschaftsleistung, ist aber vor allem bekannt als Produzent von Wein und Sekt. Zwei Drittel der deutschen Anbaufläche für Wein liegen in Rheinland-Pfalz.

🇬🇧 *The state of Rhineland-Palatinate is in the south-west of Germany next to France, Belgium and Luxembourg. The state was created in 1946 from Bavarian, Hessian and Prussian regions.*

The Roman commander Julius Caesar already built bridges across the river Rhine in the area of the present-day state. Several towns were founded in the Roman period, such as Mainz, Koblenz and Trier. During the Middle Ages, numerous castles were built on the banks of the rivers Rhine and Moselle.

Although a powerful economic state, Rhineland-Palatinate is mainly known as producer of wine and champagne. Two-thirds of the German wine growing areas are within the boundaries of the Rhineland-Palatinate.

Mainz
Mainz

Landeshauptstadt von Rheinland-Pfalz	
Fläche:	98 km²
Einwohner:	196 000
Capital of Rhineland-Palatinate	
Area:	*38 sq miles*
Inhabitants:	*196,000*

► Das Gutenberg-Denkmal auf dem Gutenberg-Platz in der Nähe des Mainzer Doms erinnert an den Erfinder des Buchdrucks.

► *The Gutenberg monument at Gutenberg Square in the vicinity of Mainz cathedral remembers the inventor of the letter press.*

◄ Die Theodor-Heuss-Brücke verbindet die rheinland-pfälzische Landeshauptstadt Mainz mit der hessischen Landeshauptstadt Wiesbaden.

◄ *The Theodor Heuss Bridge connects Mainz, capital of Rhineland-Palatinate, with Wiesbaden, capital of Hesse.*

▬ Die Landeshauptstadt Mainz liegt am linken Ufer des Rheins an der Mündung des Mains. Gegenüber, am rechten Rheinufer, liegt Wiesbaden. In der Gegend um Mainz finden sich Spuren eiszeitlicher Jäger und Siedlungsreste der Kelten. Die Gründung der Stadt erfolgte kurz vor der Zeitenwende durch die Römer. Vermutlich noch in der Endphase des römischen Reichs erhielt Mainz einen christlichen Bischof.

Der wohl berühmteste Mainzer Bürger war Johannes Gutenberg, der um 1450 den Buchdruck mit beweglichen Lettern erfand. Ein Exemplar seiner von ihm gedruckten Bibel kann im Gutenberg-Museum in Mainz besichtigt werden.

Zu den traditionsreichsten und größten Veranstaltungen in Mainz gehört die Mainzer Fastnacht. Nach dem christlichen Kalender beginnt in der Nacht zum Aschermittwoch die Fastenzeit.

🇬🇧 *The capital Mainz is on the left bank of the river Rhine where the river Main joins the Rhine. On the opposite side of the Rhine is Wiesbaden. Signs of ice-age hunters and remains of Celtic settlements have been found in the area around Mainz. The town was founded by the Romans. Probably towards the end of the Roman Empire, Mainz became the residence of a Christian bishop.*

Certainly the most famous citizen of Mainz was Johannes Gutenberg, who invented the letter press with movable characters in about 1450. One original printed copy of his Bible is exhibited in the Gutenberg Museum of Mainz.

One of the greatest traditional events is the carnival Mainzer Fastnacht. According to the Christian calendar, the Lent begins in the night before Ash Wednesday (this is where the name Fastnacht comes from).

▼ Der 975 begonnene Dom St. Martin wurde in seiner 1000-jährigen Geschichte sieben Mal durch Feuer zerstört.

▼ *In its 1000 years history, the cathedral St. Martin, founded in 975, was destroyed by fire seven times.*

Trier
Trier

Im Westen von Rheinland-Pfalz, nahe der Grenze zu Luxemburg, liegt an der Mosel die vielleicht älteste Stadt Deutschlands. Trier war bereits zur Zeit der Römer vor über 2000 Jahren nicht nur eine militärische Ansiedlung, sondern eine Stadt mit Steinbauten und einem Amphitheater. Über die Mosel führt eine von den Römern erbaute, aber später modifizierte und restaurierte Steinbrücke, die bis zum Beginn des 20. Jahrhunderts die einzige Flussüberquerung in Trier blieb.

In the west of Rhineland-Palatinate, close to Luxembourg on the banks of the river Moselle, is one of the oldest towns of Germany. Already more than 2,000 years ago, Trier was not only a Roman military base, but also a town with buildings from stone and with an amphitheatre. The river Moselle is crossed by a stone bridge, which was constructed by the Romans and later on was modified. Up to the 20th century, this bridge was the only way across the river in Trier.

Die Porta Nigra aus dem Jahr 180 n. Chr. war ein römisches Stadttor und ist heute ein Wahrzeichen von Trier.

The Porta Nigra built in about 180 AD was a Roman town gate and is today a symbol of Trier.

Koblenz
Koblenz

Koblenz, die drittgrößte Stadt in Rheinland-Pfalz, liegt an der Mündung der Mosel in den Rhein. Der Mündungsbereich, der 1216 in den Besitz der Ritter des Deutschen Ordens überging, wird seither „Deutsches Eck" genannt und gehört heute zum UNESCO-Weltkulturerbe ebenso wie die historische Altstadt, das Kurfürstliche Schloss, Schloss Stolzenfels, die Alte Burg oder die ehemaligen preußischen Festungen.

Koblenz is the third largest town in the state and is located where the river Moselle joins the Rhine. In 1216, the place of the confluence was given to the Teutonic Knights and since that time it has been called "Deutsches Eck" (German Corner). This place as well as the historical town centre and some palaces such as the Kurfürstliche Schloss (Elector's Palace) are cultural world heritage sites.

◄ Am Zusammenfluss von Rhein und Mosel, dem Deutschen Eck, liegt Koblenz, eine der ältesten Städte Deutschlands.

◄ *Close to the German Corner where the river Moselle joins the Rhine is Koblenz, one of the oldest towns in Germany.*

Idar-Oberstein
Idar-Oberstein

Die Stadt Idar-Oberstein in der Mitte von Rheinland-Pfalz ist als Edelsteinstadt bekannt. Auswanderer aus Idar-Oberstein entdeckten in Brasilien große Achatvorkommen und schickten im Jahr 1834 erste Lieferungen in die Heimat. Die brasilianischen Achate ließen sich besser zu Schmuck verarbeiten als die heimischen Achate und lösten die Entwicklung der Stadt zum deutschen Edelsteinzentrum aus.

The town of Idar-Oberstein, which is in the middle of Rhineland-Palatinate, is well known as the town of precious stones. In 1834, emigrants from Idar-Oberstein discovered major agate deposits in Brazil and sent samples back home. The Brazilian agates proved to be better for jewellery manufacturing than the native agates. This initiated the development of the town into the German centre for precious stones.

► Einer Sage nach wurde diese Felsenkirche im Jahr 1484 von einem reumütigen Mörder erbaut.

► *According to a saga, this chapel on the rocks was founded in 1484 by a remorseful murderer.*

Worms
Worms

▬ Gut 40 km südlich von Mainz liegt am Rhein die Stadt Worms, die neben Trier und Köln ebenfalls den Titel „älteste Stadt Deutschlands" beansprucht. Seit dem frühen Mittelalter wurden in Worms immer wieder Reichstage der Kaiser abgehalten, unter anderem 1521, als Martin Luther seine reformatorischen Thesen vor Kaiser Karl V. verteidigte. Worms ist auch bekannt als ein zentraler Schauplatz der Nibelungensage.

⚑ *About 25 miles south of Mainz, on the banks of the river Rhine is the town of Worms, which is also one of the oldest towns in Germany. Since the early Middle Ages, many Imperial Diets were held in Worms, as in 1521, when Martin Luther defended his reforming statements in the presence of Emperor Karl V. Worms is also a central scene of the legend of the Nibelungs.*

⚐ Seit über 1000 Jahren ist der Kaiserdom St. Peter ein Wahrzeichen von Worms.

⚐ *For more than 1,000 years, the Emperor's Cathedral St. Peter has been a symbol of Worms.*

Speyer
Speyer

▬ Im Süden von Rheinland-Pfalz liegt am linken Rheinufer die Stadt Speyer. Hier hatten die Römer eines ihrer Kastelle entlang des Rheins errichtet. Vermutlich im 4., spätestens im 7. Jahrhundert war Speyer Bischofssitz. Im 11. Jahrhundert wurde der Mariendom errichtet, der nach dem Willen des Kaisers Konrad II. die größte Kirche des Abendlandes werden sollte. Unter seinem Enkel Heinrich IV. wurde der Dom 1106 eingeweiht.

⚑ *In the south of the state, on the left bank of the river Rhine, is the town of Speyer, where the Romans had built one of their Rhine fortresses. Probably in the 4th century, at the latest in the 7th century, Speyer was the seat of a diocese. The cathedral St. Maria was built in the 11th century and was intended by Emperor Konrad II to become the largest church of the Occident. In 1106 the cathedral was inaugurated.*

◄ Der Kaiserdom von Speyer, in dem zwölf Kaiser, Könige und Königinnen beigesetzt sind

◄ *The imperial cathedral of Speyer where twelve emperors, kings and queens are buried*

Ludwigshafen
Ludwigshafen

▬ Ludwigshafen am Rhein ist nach Mainz die zweitgrößte Stadt in Rheinland-Pfalz – aber gleichzeitig eine der jüngsten. Im Jahr 1609 wurde von der Festung Mannheim rechts des Rheins ein Brückenkopf, die „Mannheimer Rheinschanze", am linken Rheinufer errichtet. Hier entstand später eine Siedlung, die 1843 zu Ehren des Landesherrn, des Bayernkönigs Ludwig I., den Namen Ludwigshafen erhielt.

Das zu Bayern gehörende Ludwigshafen wurde als „Konkurrent" zum badischen Mannheim sehr gefördert und erhielt 1859 die Stadtrechte. 1865 siedelte sich die „Badische Anilin- und Sodafabrik" in Ludwigshafen an, weil der Mannheimer Gemeinderat der Firma kein Gelände zur Verfügung stellte. Seitdem hat sich Ludwigshafen zu einem wichtigen Standort insbesondere der chemischen und pharmazeutischen Industrie entwickelt. Dabei spielte auch der Rhein als Wasserstraße eine bedeutende Rolle.

🇬🇧 *Ludwigshafen on the Rhine is the second largest city of Rhineland-Palatinate and is simultaneously one of the youngest towns. In 1609, the fortress of Mannheim on the right bank of the Rhine built a bridgehead on the left bank, the so-called "Mannheimer Rheinschanze". A settlement arose in this place. In 1843, it received the name Ludwigshafen honouring the ruler Ludwig I, king of Bavaria.*

The Bavarian Ludwigshafen was strongly promoted as a competitor to Mannheim, which belonged to Baden, and received its town charter in 1859. In 1865, the "Badische Anilin- und Sodafabrik" (BASF) moved to Ludwigshafen, after the Mannheim city council had not been able to provide land for the factory. Since then, Ludwigshafen has developed into a major site of the chemical and pharmaceutical industry. The Rhine plays an important role as a waterway.

⍔ Das Wilhelm-Hack-Museum wurde 1971 von dem Kölner Kaufmann Wilhelm Hack gestiftet. Die Fassade ist ein Entwurf von Joan Miró.

⍔ *The Wilhelm Hack Museum was donated in 1971 by the Cologne businessman Wilhelm Hack. Its facade was designed by Joan Miró.*

Nürburgring
Nürburgring

In der Eifel, im äußersten Norden von Rheinland-Pfalz, liegt der Nürburgring, eine legendäre Rennstrecke, die 1927 eingeweiht wurde. Die ursprüngliche Länge der Rundstrecke betrug insgesamt etwa 28 km und wurde bis 1982 für Grand-Prix-Automobilrennen genutzt. Seit 1984 werden die Formel-1-Rennen auf einem neuen, 5,148 km langen Rundkurs ausgetragen. Dem alten und neuen Streckenverlauf ist noch die Start- und Zielgerade gemeinsam.

In the Eifel Mountains, in the very north of Rhineland-Palatinate, is the Nürburgring, the legendary motor sport race track which was opened in 1927. Originally, the track length was 17.6 miles and was used for Grand Prix car races until 1982. Since 1984, Formula One races have been started on the new 2.8-miles race track. However, the old and the new race track have the start-finish area in common.

▼ Der legendäre Nürburgring ist eine der beliebtesten Rennstrecken der Welt.

▼ *The legendary Nürburgring ist one of the most popular race tracks of the world.*

Kaiserslautern
Kaiserslautern

▬ Das Gebiet des Pfälzer Waldes im Süden des Landes war bereits in der Steinzeit besiedelt. Im 12. Jahrhundert errichtete Kaiser Barbarossa hier eine Pfalz, das heißt, einen kaiserlichen Stützpunkt. Aus diesem Umstand und aus dem Ortsnamen Lautern bildete sich im 14. Jahrhundert der Name Kaiserslautern mit dem Beinamen „Barbarossastadt". Der Pfälzer Wald bildet zusammen mit einem Waldgebiet der französischen Vogesen das grenzüberschreitende UNESCO-Biosphärenreservat Pfälzerwald-Vosges du Nord.

🇬🇧 *The region of the Palatinate Forest in the south of the state was settled in the Iron Age already. In the 12th century, Emperor Barbarossa built a Palatinate palace in this area. From this event as well as from the name of a village, Lautern, the town name Kaiserslautern was derived in the 14th century with the second name "Town of Barbarossa". Both the Palatinate Forest and a forest area of the French Vosges form the UNESCO biosphere reserve Palatinate Forest-Vosges du Nord.*

◄ Der im Jahr 2000 eröffnete Japanische Garten resultiert aus der Partnerschaft zu der japanischen Stadt Bunkyoku.

◄ *The Japanese Garden opened in 2000 and is a result of the friendship with the Japanese city of Bunkyoku.*

Deutsche Weinstraße
German Wine Route

▬ Die Deutsche Weinstraße durchzieht auf einer Länge von 85 km das zweitgrößte Weinanbaugebiet Deutschlands. Die Straße im Süden beginnt an der Grenze zum Französischen Elsass und passiert in Richtung Norden die Weinbaugemeinden mit den berühmtesten Lagen in Deidesheim, Forst und Wachenheim. Ein vom Klima besonders begünstigter Ort ist das malerische Deidesheim, wo sogar Südfrüchte reifen.

🇬🇧 *The 53-mile-long German Wine Route runs through the second largest wine growing area in Germany. The route starts in the south at the border to French Alsace and goes towards the north, passing the viniculture towns with the most famous vineyards in Deidesheim, Forst and Wachenheim. The picturesque town Deidesheim is favoured by the climate in such a way that tropical fruits may ripen.*

▲ Die Gemeinde Dernau an der Weinstraße geht vermutlich auf eine römische Siedlung zurück.

▲ *The township of Dernau at the German Wine Route probably originated from a Roman settlement.*

Rhein
River Rhine

■ Der Rhein ist die am stärksten befahrene Wasserstraße Europas. Er hat eine Gesamtlänge von über 1300 km. Weit mehr als die Hälfte davon ist für die Berufsschifffahrt nutzbar. Das Quellgebiet des Rheins liegt überwiegend im schweizerischen Graubünden. Nachdem er den Bodensee durchflossen hat, bildet der Rhein streckenweise – bis etwa Basel – die Grenze zur Schweiz. Anschließend liegt links des Stroms das französische Elsass. Kurz vor Karlsruhe endet der Grenzverlauf am Rhein.

Der Abschnitt zwischen Straßburg und Bingen wird als Oberrhein und der weitere Abschnitt bis Bonn als Mittelrhein bezeichnet. Daran schließt sich der Bereich Niederrhein an, der bis ins niederländische Mündungsgebiet reicht.

Bereits seit der Römerzeit ist der Rhein eine bedeutende Wasser- und Handelsstraße. Viele der zahllosen Burgen am Rhein verdankten ihre Existenz der Schifffahrt auf dem Rhein, nicht zuletzt durch die Einnahme von Zöllen.

▼ Rhein in Flammen: Die Ursprünge dieses traditionellen, 26 km langen Feuerzaubers gehen auf die 1930er-Jahre zurück.

▼ *Rhine going up in flames: The history of this traditional event – at a length of 18 miles – goes back to the 1930s.*

※ *The river Rhine is the most used waterway in Europe. Its total length is 808 miles. More than half of this is a navigable waterway. The Rhine,s origins are in the Swiss Alps in the canton of Graubünden. After running through Lake Constance, the Rhine forms, at some locations, the frontier between Germany and Switzerland. Past Basel, left of the river is French Alsace. Close to Karlsruhe, the Rhine enters Germany exclusively.*

The section between Strasbourg and Bingen is called Upper Rhine, whereas the subsequent section down to Bonn is the Middle Rhine, which is followed by the Lower Rhine, running into the Netherlands, where the river then splits into three tributaries.

Since the days of the Romans, the Rhine has been an important waterway and trading route. Many of the countless castles along the Rhine owe their existence to the Rhine shipping, not least because of collecting tolls.

Mosel
River Moselle

▮ Die Mosel ist der größte deutsche Nebenfluss des Rheins und eine wichtige Schifffahrtsstraße. Sie entspringt in den französischen Vogesen, passiert die Stadt Metz in Lothringen und markiert vom luxemburgischen Schengen bis in die Nähe von Trier die Grenze zwischen Deutschland und Luxemburg. Ab Trier fließt die Mosel in vielen Schleifen, Mäandern, nach Nordosten und mündet am Deutschen Eck in Koblenz in den Rhein. Dabei führt sie dem Rhein mehr Wasser zu als der Main.

Die Landschaft an der Mosel ist von den zum Teil sehr steilen Schieferhängen geprägt, an denen Wein angebaut wird. Die Weinberge an der Mosel liefern vor allem Rieslingweine von hoher Qualität. Im Moseltal führen die Moselweinstraße und der Mosel-Radweg von Metz bis nach Koblenz. Über dem Tal verläuft der Moselhöhen-Wanderweg, von dem aus man auch den steilsten Weinberg Europas begehen kann.

▮ Zell an der Mosel lockt mit seinem milden Klima und seinem guten Wein Touristen aus aller Welt an.

▮ *The town of Zell on the river Moselle, its mild climate and its fine wine attract tourists from all over the world.*

▮ *The river Moselle is the largest German tributary of the Rhine and an important waterway. It rises in the French Vosges and passes the town of Metz in Lorraine. From Schengen in Luxembourg to the area of Trier, the river forms the border between Germany and Luxembourg. Past Trier, the Moselle runs towards the north-east with many meanders and joins the river Rhine at Deutsches Eck (German Corner) in Koblenz. Its discharge is larger than that of the river Mainz.*

The landscape along the Moselle is characterized by partly very steep slopes of slate, where wine is cultivated. The Moselle vineyards supply especially white Riesling grapes of high quality. Along the Moselle valley, the Moselle wine route and the Moselle bicycle path run from Metz to Koblenz. Above the valley is the long distance path, the so-called "Moselhöhen-Wanderweg", which leads to the steepest vineyard in Europe.

Saarland
Saarland

▼ Der Aussichtspunkt Cloef bei Orscholz bietet einen grandiosen Blick auf die Große Saarschleife.

▼ *The location Cloef close to the town of Orscholz offers a great view down to the Bend in the Saar.*

Lage:	im Südwesten Deutschlands
Fläche:	2 600 km²
Einwohner:	1,05 Millionen
Landeshauptstadt:	Saarbrücken
Position:	*in the south-west of Germany*
Area:	*1,000 sq miles*
Inhabitants:	*1.05 million*
Capital:	*Saarbrücken*

Das Saarland liegt im Südwesten Deutschlands und grenzt an die Staaten Frankreich und Luxemburg, auf deutscher Seite aber nur an das Bundesland Rheinland-Pfalz. Etwa seit dem 17. Jahrhundert wechselte die Herrschaft über das Gebiet mehrfach. Dabei wurde das Saarland gewissermaßen abwechselnd ein französisches Departement oder eine deutsche Provinz. Im Jahr 1957 wurde das Saarland nach einer Volksabstimmung das zehnte Land der Bundesrepublik.

139

Wegen seiner ehemals sehr reichen Steinkohlevorkommen wurde das Saarland im 19. und 20. Jahrhundert ein außerordentlich wichtiges Zentrum der Kohle- und Stahlindustrie. Heute sind die wirtschaftlich abbaubaren Vorkommen weitgehend erschöpft.

The state of Saarland in the south-west of Germany borders on both France and Luxembourg, but only on one German state, Rhineland-Palatinate. Since the 17th century, the region has been alternately under different rules. Saarland was several times a French department as well as a German province. In 1957, after a plebiscite, Saarland became a state of the Federal Republic.

Because of its once rich hard coal deposits Saarland developed in the 19th and 20th century into an extraordinarily important centre of the coal and steel industry. Today, the economically exploitable deposits have been almost completely mined.

Saarbrücken
Saarbrücken

Landeshauptstadt des Saarlands	
Fläche:	167 km²
Einwohner:	181 000
Capital of Saarland	
Area:	*65 sq miles*
Inhabitants:	*181,000*

► Die 1775 vollendete Ludwigskirche ist eine der bedeutendsten Barockbauten in Deutschland und das Wahrzeichen der Stadt Saarbrücken.

► *The church Ludwigskirche, finished in 1775, is one of the most important buildings of the Baroque and a symbol of the city of Saarbrücken.*

◄ Das Alte Rathaus am Schlossplatz in Saarbrücken wurde 1897 bis 1900 erbaut. Besonders sehenswert ist der Festsaal des Rathauses.

◄ *The Old Townhall at the Saarbrücken square Schlossplatz was built from 1897 to 1900. Worth seeing is the ballroom of the townhall.*

🇩🇪 Der Name Saarbrücken leitet sich von einer Königsburg ab, die vor rund 1000 Jahren Kaiser Otto III. dem Bistum Metz schenkte. Ab der Mitte des 18. Jahrhunderts erlebte Saarbrücken durch den Steinkohlebergbau und das industrielle Schmelzen von Eisen einen großen wirtschaftlichen Aufschwung. In dieser Zeit entstanden das Residenzschloss, die Ludwigskirche und zahlreiche weitere barocke Prachtbauten, die Saarbrücken zu einer geschlossenen Barockstadt machten.

Mit dem weitgehenden Rückgang des Kohlebergbaus waren größere Umstrukturierungen verbunden. Die Industrie rund um Kohle und Stahl verlor an Bedeutung und im Dienstleistungsbereich entstanden neue Arbeitsplätze. In den letzten Jahren wurde Saarbrücken ein Zentrum der Informatik, sowohl in der Forschung als auch in der industriellen Umsetzung. Hier befindet sich das weltweit größte Forschungszentrum für Künstliche Intelligenz.

🇬🇧 *The name Saarbrücken is derived from a royal castle, which was given by Emperor Otto III to the diocese of Metz 1000 years ago. From the middle of the 18th century, the town of Saarbrücken enjoyed a great upturn caused by both coal mining and industrial smelting of iron ore. This was the time when the palace Residenzschloss, the church Ludwigskirche and some more magnificent Baroque buildings were built, which made Saarbrücken a complete Baroque town.*

The far-reaching decrease of coal mining caused major restructuring programs. The coal and steel industry lost much of its importance and was replaced by service enterprises. During the last years, Saarbrücken has developed into a centre of information technologies, both in research and in industrial application. Saarbrücken houses the worldwide largest research centre for artificial intelligence.

Saarlouis
Saarlouis

🇩🇪 Die Stadt Saarlouis liegt etwa 25 km nordwestlich von Saarbrücken an der Saar. Der Name – ursprünglich Sarre-Louis – stammt von ihrem Gründer, dem französischen König Ludwig XIV. (frz. Louis XIV.), der hier im Jahr 1680 eine Festung errichten ließ. Das Stadtwappen mit der aufgehenden Sonne und den drei bourbonischen Lilien wurde der Stadt 1683 vom „Sonnenkönig" verliehen. Die ehemalige Festung bestimmt auch heute noch den sechseckigen Grundriss der Innenstadt.

🇬🇧 *The city of Saarlouis on the banks of the river Saar is about 15 miles north-west of Saarbrücken. Its name is derived from its founder, the French King Louis XIV, who ordered the building of a fortress at this place in 1680. The municipal coat of arms, which includes a rising sun and three Bourbon lilies, was granted by "The Sun King" himself. The former fortress still dominates the hexagonal ground plan of the city centre.*

▲ Die ehemalige Festung der Stadt bestimmt auch heute noch den sechseckigen Grundriss der Innenstadt.

▲ *The former fortress of the town still dominates the hexagonal ground plan of the town centre.*

Neunkirchen
Neunkirchen

▬ Neunkirchen, etwa 20 km nordöstlich von Saarbrücken, ist die zweitgrößte Stadt des Saarlands. Bereits im späten 17. Jahrhundert wurden die Kohlevorkommen der Region erschlossen. Gleichzeitig wurde Eisenerz aus Lothringen eingeführt und geschmolzen. So entstand in Neunkirchen eine bedeutende Eisenindustrie – bis vor einigen Jahrzehnten. Im Jahr 1968 wurde die letzte Kohlengrube und 1982 das Eisenwerk geschlossen.

► Ein Industriedenkmal ist das Alte Hütten-Areal in Neunkirchen, ein ehemaliges Eisenwerk, das zu einem Freizeit- und Kulturzentrum umgestaltet wurde.

► *The Alte Hütten-Areal, a former ironworks, is an industrial monument which has been changed into a centre for leisure and cultural activities.*

❖ *Neunkirchen, which is 12 miles north-east of Saarbrücken, is the second largest town of Saarland. The coal deposits of the region were exploited already in the late 17th century. At the same time iron ore was imported from Lorraine and smelted. So an important steel industry arose in Neunkirchen – up to a few decades ago. In 1968, the last coal mine and in 1982 the last ironworks were closed.*

Saar
River Saar

▬ Das Quellgebiet der Saar liegt in den französischen Vogesen. Südlich von Saarbrücken erreicht die Saar das Saarland und mündet bei Konz in Rheinland-Pfalz in die Mosel. Bei Mettlach – kurz bevor der Fluss das Saarland wieder verlässt – befindet sich die sehenswerte Große Saarschleife. Der untere Abschnitt der Saar bis zur Mündung in die Mosel ist vom Weinanbau geprägt.

❖ *The origins of the river Saar are in the French Vosges. South of Saarbrücken, the river enters Saarland and joins the river Moselle near Konz in Rhineland-Palatinate. Near the village of Mettlach – just before the river leaves Saarland – is the impressive Große Saarschleife (Bend in the Saar). The lower section of the Saar down to the river Moselle is characterized by viniculture.*

◄ Wenige Kilometer von Mettlach entfernt ändert die Saar ihre Richtung um 180 Grad. Die Große Saarschleife begeistert jedes Jahr unzählige Besucher.

◄ *Only a few miles from the town of Mettlach, the river Saar makes a U-turn. The so-called Bend in the Saar, or Große Saarschleife, attracts countless visitors every year.*

Industrie
Industrie

◼ Der historische Schwerpunkt der Industrie im Saarland liegt beim Kohlebergbau. Der planmäßige Abbau der Steinkohle begann im 18. Jahrhundert und erreichte seinen Höhepunkt noch vor der Mitte des 20. Jahrhunderts. Um die Transportwege für die Kohle kurz zu halten, siedelten sich die größten Energieverbraucher, die Eisenhütten, in der Nähe der Bergwerke an. So gehörte das Saarland nicht nur zu den bedeutendsten europäischen Steinkohlerevieren, sondern auch zu den wichtigsten Stahlproduzenten.

Mit der Schließung der nicht mehr wirtschaftlich nutzbaren Kohlegruben ging auch die Eisenproduktion in den letzten Jahrzehnten zurück. Heute fördert nur noch ein Bergwerk mit knapp 4000 Mitarbeitern etwa 3,6 Millionen Tonnen Kohle jährlich. Der letzte Hochofen wurde 1986 stillgelegt und gehört zum UNESCO-Weltkulturerbe „Völklinger Hütte". Die Stahl verarbeitende Industrie, auch die Autoindustrie, ist im Saarland jedoch stark vertreten.

⊞ *The historical focal point of Saarland is coal mining. The controlled exploitation of hard coal started in the 18th century and reached its peak before the middle of the 20th century. In order to keep transportation distances short, the major energy consumers, which were the ironworks, settled close to the coal mines. This is why Saarland was not only one of the most significant hard coal regions but also one of the most important steel producers.*

With the shut down of uneconomic coal mines the production of iron decreased in the past decades, too. Today, only one mine with about 4,000 employees is left, which mines about 3.6 million metric tons per year. The last blast furnace was closed in 1986 and is now the UNESCO cultural world heritage site "Völklinger Hütte". The steel working industry, like the motorcar industry, however, is well represented in Saarland.

▼ Die Völklinger Hütte, einst eines der bedeutendsten Stahlwerke in Europa, wurde 1986 stillgelegt und 1994 zum Weltkulturerbe erklärt.

▼ *The Völklinger Hütte which was one of the most important steel producers in Europe was shut down in 1986 and became a world cultural heritage site in 1994.*

143

Baden-Württemberg

Baden-Wurttemberg

Schon bald nach Ihrer Quelle muss sich die Donau einen Weg durch die Ausläufer der Schwäbischen Alb bahnen.

Soon after its origin, the Danube has to find its way through the foothills of the Swabian Jura.

144

Lage:	im Süden/Südwesten Deutschlands
Fläche:	53 700 km²
Einwohner:	10,7 Millionen
Landeshauptstadt:	Stuttgart
Position:	*in the south and south-west of Germany*
Area:	*13,784 sq miles*
Inhabitants:	*10.7 million*
Capital:	*Stuttgart*

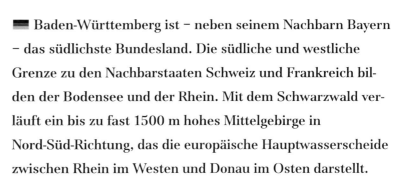 Baden-Württemberg ist – neben seinem Nachbarn Bayern – das südlichste Bundesland. Die südliche und westliche Grenze zu den Nachbarstaaten Schweiz und Frankreich bilden der Bodensee und der Rhein. Mit dem Schwarzwald verläuft ein bis zu fast 1500 m hohes Mittelgebirge in Nord-Süd-Richtung, das die europäische Hauptwasserscheide zwischen Rhein im Westen und Donau im Osten darstellt.

Baden-Württemberg zählt zu den wirtschaftsstärksten und innovativsten Regionen in Europa. Innerhalb Deutschlands gilt es als das traditionelle Land der Erfinder. Die ersten Automobile der Welt wurden hier gebaut. Heute haben viele Unternehmen der Hochtechnologie ihren Standort in Baden-Württemberg.

Baden-Wurttemberg is – alongside its neighbour Bavaria – the most southern state in Germany. The southern and western borders to Switzerland and France are formed by Lake Constance and the river Rhine. From south to north runs the Black Forest low mountain area with up to 4,900-foot-high summits which form the European main watershed with the Rhine in the west and the Danube in the east.

Baden-Wurttemberg is one of the most powerful and most innovative regions in Europe. Within Germany, it is regarded as the traditional land of inventors. The world's first motorcars were built here. Today, many high-tech companies have their headquarters in Baden-Wurttemberg.

Stuttgart
Stuttgart

Landeshauptstadt von Baden-Württemberg	
Fläche:	207 km²
Einwohner:	594 000
Capital of Baden-Wurttemberg	
Area:	*80 sq miles*
Inhabitants:	*594,000*

► Der Cannstatter Wasen ist ein ehemaliger Exerzierplatz der Stuttgarter Garnison, auf dem seit 1818 das von König Wilhelm I. gestifete Cannstatter Volksfest stattfindet.

► *The Cannstatter Wasen is a former Stuttgart garrison drill ground which since 1818 has been used for the Canstatt public festival, donated by King Wilhelm I.*

◄ Der Schlossplatz mit Sicht auf das Neue Schloss. Der Spätbarockbau ist eines der letzten großen Stadtschlösser Süddeutschlands.

◄ The square Schlossplatz with a view of the palace Neue Schloss. This building from the late Baroque is one of the last big town palaces in Southern Germany.

▬ Stuttgart liegt im Zentrum des Landes Baden-Württemberg im so genannten „Stuttgarter Kessel" zwischen mehreren Hügeln. Während das Gebiet schon um die Zeitenwende besiedelt war, fand die eigentliche Gründung Stuttgarts vor gut 1000 Jahren statt. Im 13. Jahrhundert gelangte Stuttgart in den Besitz des späteren Königreichs Württemberg und wurde Residenzstadt. Herzog Carl Eugen von Württemberg ließ 1746 mit dem Neuen Schloss die letzte große barocke Residenzschlossanlage in Deutschland erbauen.

Die jüngere Geschichte Stuttgarts prägten Erfinder und Pioniere der Technik, zum Beispiel Gottlieb Daimler, Wilhelm Maybach, Robert Bosch oder Ferdinand Porsche. Heute befinden sich im Ballungsraum Stuttgart nicht nur zwei führende Hersteller der Automobilbranche, sondern auch bedeutende High-Tech-Unternehmen der Elektronik und Informatik.

▓ *Stuttgart is in the middle of the state, in the so-called Stuttgart Basin between several hills. While the region was populated already 2000 years ago, the actual foundation of Stuttgart was in the 10th century. In the 13th century, Stuttgart became part of the later kingdom of Wurttemberg and became its residence town. In 1746, Duke Carl Eugen of Wurttemberg ordered the building of the palace Neues Schloss, which is the most recent large Baroque residence in Germany.*

The more recent history of Stuttgart is characterized by inventors and technical pioneers such as Gottlieb Daimler, Wilhelm Maybach, Robert Bosch or Ferdinand Porsche. Within the conurbation area of Stuttgart are not only two leading producers of motorcars but also a number of important high-tech plants of the electronic and information industry.

▼ Der Wallberg in Pforzheim wurde aus Trümmerschutt des Zweiten Weltkriegs künstlich angelegt. Auf seiner Kuppe mahnen Stelen zum Frieden.

▼ The Wallberg in Pforzheim is an artificial mountain of rubble left from World War II. On its top, several steles remind of peace.

Pforzheim
Pforzheim

▬ Die „Goldstadt" Pforzheim liegt knapp 40 km nordwestlich von Stuttgart. Die Stadt entwickelte sich aus einer römischen Siedlung am Zusammenfluss dreier Flüsse, auf denen Holz aus dem südlich von Pforzheim gelegenen Schwarzwald transportiert wurde. Mit der 1768 gegründeten Goldschmiedeschule begann der Aufstieg Pforzheims als Zentrum der deutschen Schmuck- und Silberwarenindustrie. Zeitweise, etwa um 1913, war die Hälfte der Pforzheimer Bevölkerung in der Schmuck- und Uhrenindustrie beschäftigt.

▓ *Pforzheim, the "Town of Gold", is about 25 miles northwest of Stuttgart. The town developed from a Roman settlement at a place where three rivers are joining, which had been used as waterways carrying wood from the Black Forest south of Pforzheim. A goldsmith's school founded in 1768 initiated the development of Pforzheim into the centre of the German jewellery and silver industry. For some periods around 1913, half of all inhabitants were engaged in the jewellery and watch industry.*

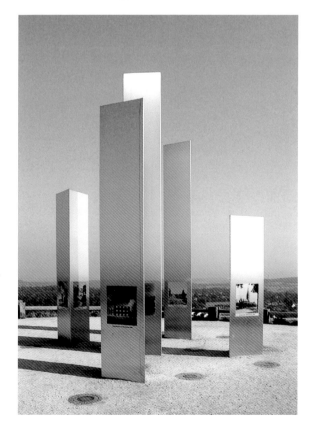

Heidelberg
Heidelberg

▬ Die ehemalige kurpfälzische Residenzstadt Heidelberg am Neckar ist einer der von Touristen aus aller Welt meistbesuchten Orte in Deutschland. Die im Jahr 1386 gegründete Universität Heidelberg ist die älteste Hochschule der Bundesrepublik. Im Schloss oberhalb der historischen Altstadt kann man das 1751 vollendete Große Fass besichtigen, das vermutlich größte Weinfass der Welt. Es kann 220 000 Liter Wein aufnehmen.

✱ *The former Elector's residence town Heidelberg on the banks of the river Neckar is one of the most frequently visited places in Germany. The University of Heidelberg, founded in 1386, is the oldest one in Germany. The palace above the historical town centre houses the Große Fass from 1751, which is probably the world's largest wine-cask. Its capacity is 220,000 litres of wine.*

▲ Das Schloss Heidelberg über dem Neckartal wurde 1693 zerstört und nie wieder vollständig aufgebaut.

▲ *The castle of Heidelberg above the Neckar valley was destroyed in 1693 and was never again completely rebuilt.*

148

▼ Durch die Weinberge um Heilbronn verläuft der Wein-Panorama-Weg, ein Museum unter freiem Himmel.

▼ *Like an open air museum, the path Wein-Panorama-Weg leads through the vineyards of Heilbronn.*

Heilbronn
Heilbronn

▬ Nördlich von Stuttgart – und ebenfalls am Neckar – liegt die Stadt Heilbronn, die von einer ausgedehnten Weinberglandschaft umgeben ist. Der Weinbau hat in Heilbronn eine große Tradition und ist bis heute ein wichtiger Wirtschaftsfaktor geblieben. Seit 1815 bis in die Gegenwart wurde der Neckar als Wasserstraße ausgebaut. Heute gehört der Heilbronner Kanalhafen zu den größten deutschen Binnenhäfen.

✱ *North of Stuttgart – on the banks of the river Neckar, too – is the town of Heilbronn, which is surrounded by a widespread landscape of vineyards. Viniculture has an old tradition in Heilbronn and still is an important economic factor today. From 1815 until the present time, the Neckar was and is being enlarged as a waterway. Today the Heilbronn Canal Port is one of the largest river ports in Germany.*

Karlsruhe
Karlsruhe

■ Die Stadt Karlsruhe entstand am 17. Juni 1715, als der Grundstein für ein Schloss des Markgrafen von Baden-Durlach, Karl-Wilhelm, gelegt wurde. Um das Schloss als Zentrum wurden nach genauen Plänen strahlenförmig 32 Straßen angelegt, die heute noch im Stadtbild zu erkennen sind. Von Beginn an war Karlsruhe Residenzstadt. Das Bundesverfassungsgericht und der Bundesgerichtshof haben ihren Sitz in Karlsruhe.

▨ *The city of Karlsruhe was founded on June 17, 1715, when Karl-Wilhelm, Margrave of Baden-Durlach laid the foundation stone for a palace. With the palace as the focal point, 32 streets were exactly planned to radiate out, which still can be seen from today's city map. From its beginning, Karlsruhe was a residence town, which today houses both the Federal Constitutional Court and the Federal Supreme Court.*

⏶ Als exakter Mittelpunkt von Karlsruhe wurde das Schloss geplant und gebaut.

⏶ *The palace of Karlsruhe was planned and built exactly in the centre of the city.*

149

⏷ In der Trinkhalle des Kurorts von 1842 wurden früher Heilwasser und frisch gepresster Traubensaft ausgeschenkt.

⏷ *The spa's drinking hall of 1842 was used in former times to serve medical water and freshly squeezed grape juice.*

Baden-Baden
Baden-Baden

■ In der Oberrheinischen Tiefebene, am Nordwestrand des Schwarzwalds, liegt die Kurstadt Baden-Baden, deren heiße Quellen schon die Römer zu schätzen wussten. Seit dem frühen 19. Jahrhundert genießt Baden-Baden als Kurort Weltruf. Im Jahr 1748 erhielt die Stadt die Konzession zum Glücksspiel. Auch der russische Dichter Dostojewski spielte in Baden-Baden, was sich in seinem Roman „Der Spieler" niederschlug.

▨ *The spa Baden-Baden is in the Upper Rhine lowland at the north-western edge of the Black Forest. Already the Romans enjoyed its hot springs. Since the early 19th century, Baden-Baden has been a spa of world fame. In 1748, the town received the licence for gaming. Even the Russian poet Dostojewski gambled in Baden-Baden, which is recorded in his novel "The Gambler".*

Tübingen
Tübingen

▬ Etwa 40 km südlich von Stuttgart liegt die traditionsreiche Universitätsstadt Tübingen. Der wohl bekannteste Tübinger Professor war Papst Benedikt XVI. (Joseph Ratzinger), der von 1966 bis 1969 einen Lehrstuhl für katholische Dogmatik innehatte. Im Jahr 1971 wurde die Kunsthalle Tübingen gegründet, die mit Ausstellungen berühmter Maler wie Paul Cézanne oder Pablo Picasso große Beachtung findet.

🇬🇧 *About 25 miles south of Stuttgart is the traditional university town of Tübingen. Its probably most famous professor was Pope Benedict XVI (Joseph Ratzinger), who held a chair of catholic dogmatic theology from 1966 to 1969. In 1971, the art gallery Kunsthalle Tübingen was founded, which has received a lot of attention for its exhibitions of famous artists like Paul Cézanne or Pablo Picasso.*

▲ Der Hölderlinturm in der Tübinger Altstadt. Hier lebte der Dichter Friedrich Hölderlin von 1807 bis zu seinem Tod 1843.

▲ *The Hölderlin tower in the historical town centre of Tübingen. The poet Friedrich Hölderlin lived there from 1807 to 1843.*

150

Ulm
Ulm

▬ Im Westen von Baden-Württemberg, an der Mündung der Iller in die Donau, liegt die Stadt Ulm. Auf der rechten Seite der Iller grenzt die bayerische Stadt Neu-Ulm an. Das Ulmer Münster, die Hauptkirche der Stadt, ist die größte protestantische Kirche und besitzt den höchsten Kirchturm der Welt. Er ist 161 m hoch. Als berühmtester Sohn der Stadt gilt Albert Einstein, der 1879 hier geboren wurde.

▲ Das im 14. Jahrhundert begonnene Ulmer Münster wurde erst 513 Jahre später in seiner heutigen Form vollendet.

▲ *The cathedral of Ulm construction of which started in the 14th century was finished 513 years later.*

🇬🇧 *In the west of Baden-Wurttemberg, where the river Iller joins the Danube, is the town of Ulm. On the right bank of the river Iller, Ulm borders the Bavarian town Neu-Ulm (New Ulm). The cathedral, the main church of the town, is the largest Protestant church and has the world's highest church tower, which is 528 feet high. The most famous son of the town is probably Albert Einstein, who was born here in 1879.*

Freiburg
Freiburg

▬ Im Südwesten des Landes, am Rand des Schwarzwalds, liegt Freiburg, eine der wärmsten Großstädte Deutschlands. Die malerische Altstadt zieht jährlich drei Millionen Besucher an. Auf dem Rathausplatz mit dem Alten und Neuen Rathaus steht eine Statue des Mönchs Berthold Schwarz, der als Erfinder des Schwarzpulvers gilt. Das Leben in der Stadt wird stark durch die Universität geprägt, die einer der wichtigsten Arbeitgeber ist.

🇬🇧 *In the south-west of the state, at the edge of the Black Forest, is Freiburg. The scenic old city centre attracts three million visitors every year. On the square Rathausplatz with the old and the new town halls is a monument to the monk Berthold Schwarz, who is regarded as the inventor of gun powder. The life in the city is mainly characterized by the university, which is one of the major employers.*

▲ Das Freiburger Münster mit seiner einzigartigen, durchbrochenen Turmspitze wurde bereits im Mittelalter komplett fertiggestellt.

▲ *The cathedral of Freiburg with its unique open spire was completely finished in the Middle Ages.*

▼ Die Skulptur Imperia an der Hafeneinfahrt erinnert an die Kurtisanen zu Zeiten des Konstanzer Konzils.

▼ *The sculpture Imperia at the port is a reminder of the courtesans at the times when the coucil of Constance took place.*

Konstanz
Constance

▬ Konstanz ist die größte Stadt am Bodensee. Die Schweizer Nachbarstadt Kreuzlingen ist mit Konstanz zusammengewachsen, sodass die Staatsgrenze zwischen einzelnen Häusern und Straßen hindurch verläuft. Von 1414 bis 1418 fand das Konzil von Konstanz statt. Das Konzilsgebäude, in dem die einzige Papstwahl nördlich der Alpen stattfand, steht heute noch am Bodenseeufer in der Nähe des Hafens.

🇬🇧 *Constance is the largest town on the shore of Lake Constance. The neighbouring Swiss town Kreuzlingen is fused with Constance in such a way, that the national border runs between single houses and streets. From 1414 to 1418, the Council of Constance took place. The building, in which the only election of a pope north of the Alps took place, still exists today right on the waterfront near the port.*

Ravensburg
Ravensburg

▬ Etwa 20 km entfernt vom Bodensee liegt an einer bis ins Spätmittelalter wichtigen Handelsstraße die Stadt Ravensburg. Dank der verfügbaren Wasserkraft entstand hier 1402 eine der ersten Papiermühlen nördlich der Alpen. Auch die industrielle Entwicklung im 19. Jahrhundert stützte sich zunächst auf Wasserkraft. Ravensburg ist heute noch ein wichtiger Standort der Maschinenbaubranche.

🇬🇧 *About 12 miles from Lake Constance, at an important medieval trading route, is the city of Ravensburg. Thanks to plenty of available waterpower, one of the first paper mills north of the Alps was built in 1402. The industrial development of the 19th century was based on waterpower, too. Still today, Ravensburg is a major production site of the engineering industry.*

▲ Der weiße Turm bei St. Michael, das Wahrzeichen Ravensburgs, wird seit dem 16. Jahrhundert „Mehlsack" genannt.

▲ *The white tower of St. Michael, the symbol of Ravensburg, has been called "flour bag" since the 16th century.*

▼ Die Schlosskirche St. Marien ist ein herausragendes Beispiel des Barock am Bodensee.

▼ *The palace church St. Marien is an extraordinary example of Lake Constance Baroque.*

Insel Mainau
Mainau Island

▬ Die „Blumeninsel" Mainau ist eine kleine Insel im Bodensee, und zwar im Seebereich Überlinger See. Die Insel befindet sich im Besitz der Adelsfamilie Bernadotte, ist aber für die Öffentlichkeit zugänglich und entweder per Schiff oder zu Fuß über eine lange Brücke erreichbar. Bedingt durch das günstige Bodenseeklima wachsen im Schlosspark Palmen und andere mediterrane Pflanzen.

🇬🇧 *The "Island of Flowers", Mainau, is a small island in the western part of Lake Constance, which is called Überlinger See. The island is owned by the Bernadotte family. Nevertheless, it is open to the public. It can be reached either by ship or by foot via a long bridge. Because of the very mild climate in this area of Lake Constance, palms and other Mediterranean plants are growing in the palace's garden.*

Schwarzwald
Schwarzwald

▬ Der Schwarzwald, der fast parallel zum Oberrhein verläuft, ist Deutschlands größtes Mittelgebirge mit einer Ausdehnung von 160 km in Nord-Süd-Richtung. Der höchste Gipfel ist der Feldberg mit 1493 m Höhe. In den schönen, aber schwer zugänglichen Tälern stellten die Bauern früher im Winter die berühmten Kuckucksuhren aus Holz her. Daraus entwickelte sich im 19. Jahrhundert die Schwarzwälder Uhrenindustrie.

▨ The Black Forest, which runs almost parallel to the Upper Rhine, is the largest low mountain range in Germany. It is about 100 miles long. The highest summit Feldberg is 4,898 feet high. In former winter times, the farmers in the beautiful but hardly accessible valleys produced the famous cuckoo clocks from wood. This was the beginning of the Black Forest clock industry in the 19th century.

► Innerhalb der letzten hundert Jahre hat sich der Titisee von einem einsamen Eiszeit-Relikt zu einem touristischen Zentrum im Schwarzwald entwickelt.

► Within the last hundred years, Titisee has changed from a lonely lake of the Ice Ages into a major tourist centre of the Black Forest.

Schwäbische Alb
The Swabian Jura

▬ Die Schwäbische Alb ist ein Mittelgebirge, das an den südöstlichen Schwarzwald angrenzt und entlang der Donau auf der nördlichen Seite des Flusses verläuft. Das Gestein entstand zum großen Teil vor 150 Millionen Jahren am Boden eines Meeres. In den Sedimenten sind sehr viele Fossilien enthalten, die in den Steinbrüchen zutage treten. Berühmt geworden sind die Funde von Sauriern und Urvögeln.

▲ Die Burg Hohenzollern steht auf einem 855 m hohen, isolierten Bergkegel und war die Stammburg des Fürstengeschlechts.

▲ The Hohenzollern castle is on the top of a 2800-foot isolated mountain and was the ancestral seat of this family.

▨ The mountain range of the Swabian Jura, which borders the south-eastern part of the Black Forest, runs along the northern banks of the river Danube. Its rock strata were formed 150 million years ago from the ground of an ocean. The sediments include countless fossils which come to the light in the quarries. Among the most famous findings are dinosaurs and archaeopteryx.

Bayern
Bavaria

Blick auf den 2713 m hohen Watzmann, den
Hauptberg in den Berchtesgadener Alpen

*View to the 8900 feet Watzmann, the main
mountain in the Berchtesgadener Alps*

154

Lage:	südlichstes Bundesland Deutschlands
Fläche:	70 600 km²
Einwohner:	12,5 Millionen
Landeshauptstadt:	München
Position:	*most southern state of Germany*
Area:	*27,260 sq miles*
Inhabitants:	*12.5 million*
Capital:	*Munich*

München

■■■ Der Freistaat Bayern ist das südlichste und flächengrößte deutsche Land. Im Süden grenzt Bayern an Österreich und im Osten an Tschechien. Von 1180 bis 1918 wurde Bayern als Herzogtum und Königreich von den Wittelsbachern regiert.

Bayern hat sich in den letzten Jahrzehnten vom Agrarstaat zu einem wirtschaftlich starken Standort moderner Technologien entwickelt. Insbesondere die Automobil- und Luftfahrtindustrie sowie die Informationstechnik sind hier sehr gut vertreten. Nichtsdestoweniger ist Bayern nach wie vor die beliebteste deutsche Urlaubsregion. Vor allem die bayerischen Seen und die Alpenregionen, verbunden mit vielen Kulturdenkmälern, sind die Ziele in- und ausländischer Touristen.

155

⌗⌗ *The state of Bavaria is the most southern and, in terms of square miles, the largest state of Germany. It has borders in the south with Austria and in the east with the Czech Republic. From 1180 to 1918, Bavaria was ruled as a duchy and kingdom by the Wittelsbacher family.*

During the last decades, Bavaria has developed from an agrarian state into a powerful site of modern technologies. Especially the motorcar and aircraft industry as well as the information technologies are well represented. Nevertheless, Bavaria is still one of the most popular holiday regions. First of all, the Bavarian lakes and the Alps, in combination with cultural monuments, are the preferred destination of German and international tourists.

München
Munich

Landeshauptstadt von Bayern	
Fläche:	310 km²
Einwohner:	1 334 000
Capital of Bavaria	
Area:	*120 sq miles*
Inhabitants:	*1,334,000*

► Die Hochzeitsfeier des bayerischen Kronprinzen Ludwig am 12. Oktober 1810 war die Geburtsstunde des traditionellen Münchner Oktoberfests.

► *The wedding celebration of the Bavarian crown prince Ludwig on October 12, 1810, was the origin of the traditional Munich Oktoberfest.*

◄ Die Frauenkirche mit den beiden charakteristischen Türmen ist ein Wahrzeichen der Stadt München.

◄ *The church Frauenkirche with its characteristic twin towers is one of the symbols of Munich.*

■ Die Geschichte der Stadt München beginnt im 8. Jahrhundert, als Mönche aus dem Kloster Tegernsee bei der heutigen Peterskirche eine Niederlassung gründeten. Hieran erinnert noch der Mönch im Stadtwappen. Im Jahr 1255 wurde München Residenzstadt der Wittelsbacher. Das Schloss Nymphenburg wurde 1664 als Sommerresidenz in Auftrag gegeben. Viele Prachtbauten, die heute noch das Stadtbild beherrschen, entstanden unter König Ludwig I. von Bayern (1825–1848) und seinen Nachfolgern, die alle auch große Förderer der Künste und Wissenschaften waren. So gründete König Max II. das Maximilianeum, eine Stiftung für begabte bayerische Studenten. Das Gebäude Maximilianeum ist heute – neben der Stiftung – auch Sitz des Bayerischen Landtags. Für Wirtschaftsjournalisten ist München die deutsche Stadt mit der höchsten Wirtschaftskraft.

🇬🇧 *The history of Munich started in the 8th century, when monks from the monastery Tegernsee founded a branch at the place of the present-day church of St. Peter. The monk within the municipal coat of arms is a memento of the founders. In 1255, Munich became the residence town of the Wittelsbacher family. The palace Schloss Nymphenburg was commissioned in 1664 as their summer residence. Many magnificent buildings which characterize the present-day appearance of the city were built under the rule of King Ludwig I of Bavaria (1825–1848) and his successors, who all were great patrons of the arts and sciences. King Max II founded the endowment Maximilianeum for gifted Bavarian students. Today, the Maximilianeum building houses both the foundation itself and the Bavarian Parliament. Economic journalists classify Munich as the most powerful German city.*

▼ Das Hofbräuhaus wurde als Brauerei 1607 gegründet. Heute wird das berühmte Gebäude als Gaststätte genutzt und bietet bis zu 3000 Gästen Platz.

▼ *The Hofbräuhaus is a traditional brewery founded in 1607. Today, this famous building is used as a restaurant with a capacity of up to 3,000 guests.*

Bayreuth
Bayreuth

▬ Bayreuth, im Nordosten Bayerns, ist bekannt als die Stadt der Richard-Wagner-Festspiele. Richard Wagner besuchte 1870 Bayreuth auf der Suche nach einem Opernhaus, das für seine Werke geeignet schien. Was er suchte, fand er nicht. Aber Bayreuth bot ihm ein Grundstück außerhalb der Stadt an, um ein eigenes Festspielhaus zu errichten. Am 13. August 1876 konnte sein Festspielhaus feierlich eröffnet werden.

🇬🇧 *Bayreuth in the north-east of Bavaria is well known as the town of Richard Wagner festivals. In 1870, Richard Wagner visited Bayreuth searching for an opera theatre suitable for his operas. He did not find anything. However, the town council offered him a plot of land outside the town, where he built his festival theatre. On August 13, 1876, his festival theatre was opened.*

▼ Das Richard-Wagner-Festspielhaus wurde streng nach akustischen Gesichtspunkten erbaut. Die Innerverkleidung ist aus Holz, die Stühle haben keine Polster.

158

▼ *The Richard Wagner Opera House was designed exclusively for best acoustic conditions. This is why the inside is completely of wood with no cushions on the seats.*

Bamberg
Bamberg

▬ Im Norden von Bayern liegt die Stadt Bamberg, deren Altstadt zum UNESCO-Weltkulturerbe gehört. Sie besitzt den größten unversehrt erhaltenen historischen Stadtkern in Deutschland. Der zweite Bischof von Bamberg wurde an Weihnachten 1046 zu Papst Clemens II. gewählt, starb aber schon nach zehn Monaten Amtszeit. Er liegt im Bamberger Dom begraben. Eine lange Tradition in Bamberg haben die Brauereien mit einer großen Vielfalt an Bieren, darunter die Spezialität „Bamberger Rauchbier".

❈ *In the north of Bavaria is the town of Bamberg, whose old town centre is a UNESCO cultural heritage site. It has the largest undamaged, preserved historical town centre in Germany. On Christmas 1046, the second bishop of Bamberg was elected Pope Clemens II. However, he died already ten months later. He is buried in Bamberg cathedral. Beer brewing has a long tradition for Bamberg. Many breweries produce a large variety of types of beer, among them the special smoked beer, the so-called "Bamberger Rauchbier".*

▲ Blick über die historische Altstadt von Bamberg

▲ *View over the historical town centre of Bamberg*

159

► Die sehr alte Festung Marienberg oberhalb des Mains wurde im frühen 17. Jahrhundert in ein Renaissanceschloss umgebaut.

► *The very old fortress Marienberg on the banks of the river Main was changed into a Renaissance palace in the early 17th century.*

Würzburg
Würzburg

▬ Die 1300 Jahre alte Stadt Würzburg verdankt ihre Gründung irisch-schottischen Missionaren. Nach einem von ihnen, Kilian, ist der Würzburger Dom benannt. Die prachtvolle barocke Residenz, die zum Weltkulturerbe gehört, war Sitz der Würzburger Fürstbischöfe. An den Hängen des Mains wird von traditionsreichen Weingütern Frankenwein angebaut. Seine typische Flasche ist der oval-abgeflachte „Bocksbeutel".

❈ *The 1300 years old town of Würzburg was founded by Irish-Scottish monks. One of them, Kilian, is the patron saint of Würzburg cathedral. The magnificent Baroque residence, which is a cultural world heritage site, was the seat of the Würzburg prince-bishops. On the steep banks of the river Main, wine-growing estates of rich tradition cultivate Franconian wine. Their typical bottle is the oval flat "Bocksbeutel".*

Nürnberg
Nuremberg

▬ Nürnberg ist mit 500 000 Einwohnern die zweitgrößte Stadt Bayerns. Die Zeit um 1500 gilt als die klassische Blütezeit Nürnbergs. Berühmte Söhne der Stadt waren unter anderem der Maler Albrecht Dürer (1471–1528) und Peter Henlein, der um 1524 die Taschenuhr erfand. Zu den kulinarischen Spezialitäten Nürnbergs gehören die weltbekannten Nürnberger Lebkuchen sowie die kleinen, aber feinen Nürnberger Bratwürste.

⬚ *Nuremberg is the second largest city in Bavaria and has 500,000 inhabitants. The years around 1500 are regarded as Nuremberg's prime time. Famous sons of the city were among others the artist Albrecht Dürer (1471–1528) and Peter Henlein, who invented the pocket clock in about 1524. Culinary specialties are the world famous Lebkuchen (gingerbread) as well as the small but excellent Bratwürste (fried sausages).*

▲ Die Kaiserburg über der Altstadt von Nürnberg ist das Wahrzeichen der Stadt.

▲ *The castle Kaiserburg above the historical town centre is the symbol of Nuremberg.*

◄ Die Steinerne Brücke war 800 Jahre lang der einzige Übergang der Stadt über die Donau. Im Hintergrund der Dom St. Peter.

◄ *For a period of 800 years, the Stone Bridge was the only way across the Danube in Regensburg. The cathedral St. Peter is in the background.*

Regensburg
Regensburg

▬ Genau dort, wo die Donau in ihrem Verlauf den nördlichsten Punkt erreicht, liegt die Stadt Regensburg. Hier siedelten einige Jahrhunderte vor der Zeitenwende schon die Kelten und später die Römer. Ein Wahrzeichen Regensburgs ist die Steinerne Brücke, die etwa von 1135 bis 1146 erbaut und zum Vorbild anderer bedeutender Brücken wurde, etwa der Karlsbrücke in Prag oder der Elbebrücken in Dresden.

⬚ *The town of Regensburg is exactly where the river Danube reaches its most northern point. In this area already Celtics and in later years Romans settled. A symbol of Regensburg is its stone bridge Steinerne Brücke, which was constructed from 1135 to 1146. This bridge became the model of other significant bridges, such as the Charles Bridge in Prague or the bridges across the river Elbe in Dresden.*

Rothenburg o. T.
Rothenburg o. T.

Rothenburg ob der Tauber an der westlichen Grenze zu Baden-Württemberg ist eine kleine, fast vollständig erhaltene Stadt aus dem Mittelalter. Nach dem Ende des Dreißigjährigen Kriegs, in dem die Stadt von dem Heerführer Graf von Tilly erobert wurde, versank Rothenburg in der Bedeutungslosigkeit. Die Entwicklung der Stadt stand still. Es wurden keine Häuser mehr zerstört oder zugunsten von Neubauten abgerissen. Daher haben sich das Stadtbild und die Gebäude in ihrem damaligen Zustand so gut erhalten.

Rothenburg ist ein Anziehungspunkt für Touristen, insbesondere auch aus dem außereuropäischen Raum. Die Stadt ist auf große Touristenströme eingerichtet. Zu den regelmäßigen Veranstaltungen gehört der „Rothenburger Meistertrunk". Der Überlieferung nach soll ein Rothenburger einen Becher Wein mit 3 ¼ Litern Inhalt in einem Zug ausgetrunken haben, um den Eroberer Tilly gnädig zu stimmen.

Rothenburg ob der Tauber at the western edge of the state close to Baden-Wurttemberg is a small, almost completely preserved medieval town. After the end of the Thirty Years' War, when the town was conquered by the commander Count Tilly, Rothenburg sank into unimportance. The development of the town came to a standstill. Neither houses were destroyed anymore nor replaced by new buildings. This is why the town's appearance has been preserved so completely.

Rothenburg is a prime destination for tourists, especially from outside of Europe. The town is prepared for big numbers of tourists. One of the regular events is the "Rothenburger Meistertrunk". According to a legend, a Rothenburg citizen emptied a cup of 3 ¼ litres of wine with one gulp in order to satisfy the conqueror Tilly.

⌄ Aus der Vogelperspektive erinnert Rothenburg an ein riesiges Freilichtmuseum. Tatsächlich beherbergt die Stadt mehrere interessante Museen, darunter ein mittelalterliches Kriminalmuseum.

⌄ *A bird's-eye view of Rothenburg looks like a huge open air museum. Indeed, the town presents a number of interesting museums, besides others, a medieval crime museum.*

Augsburg
Augsburg

🏴 Die von den Römern gegründete Stadt Augsburg erlebte ihre größte Blüte in der Zeit der Renaissance. Der Kaufmann Jacob Fugger, genannt „der Reiche", finanzierte unter anderem Kriege des Kaisers und die erste Schweizergarde des Papstes. Mit der Fuggerei entstand die älteste noch heute genutzte Sozialsiedlung der Welt. 1897 hatte Rudolf Diesel in Augsburg seinen ersten funktionstüchtigen Motor fertiggestellt.

🏴 *The city of Augsburg, founded by the Romans, enjoyed its prime time during the renaissance. The businessman Jacob Fugger, called "The Rich", financed, among other things, the emperor's wars and the first Swiss Guard of the pope. He also built the Fuggerei, which is the oldest social housing estate still in service. In 1897, Rudolf Diesel finished in Augsburg his first working diesel engine.*

► Das Rathaus von Elias Holl gilt als bedeutendster Profanbau der Renaissance nördlich der Alpen.

► *The town hall is considered to be the most important Renaissance secular building north of the alps.*

Ingolstadt
Ingolstadt

🏴 Nördlich von München liegt an der Donau die Stadt Ingolstadt, in der 1516 das älteste, heute noch gültige Lebensmittelgesetz der Welt verkündet wurde: Das Reinheitsgebot für bayerisches Bier. Nach 1945 erlebte Ingolstadt eine starke wirtschaftliche Entwicklung. In der heimischen Autoindustrie hat jeder vierte Ingolstädter einen Arbeitsplatz. Ingolstadt ist auch das größte Zentrum der Erdölindustrie in Bayern.

🏴 *North of Munich, on the banks of the river Danube is the town of Ingolstadt, where the world's first food law, which is still in force, was promulgated in 1516: The purity law for Bavarian beer. After 1945, Ingolstadt enjoyed a brisk economic upturn. Every fourth citizen of Ingolstadt is engaged in the motorcar industry. The town is also the largest centre of the Bavarian oil industry.*

◄ Das Kreuztor ist eines der Wahrzeichen der Stadt Ingolstadt.

◄ *The gate Kreuztor is one of the symbols of the town of Ingolstadt.*

Landshut

Landshut

Die Stadt Landshut liegt etwa 70 km nordöstlich von München an der Isar. Die gute Verkehrsanbindung an die Landeshauptstadt ist mit ein Grund für die große Wirtschaftskraft der Stadt. Als eine Veranstaltung von überregionaler Bedeutung finden alle vier Jahre die Festspiele der „Landshuter Hochzeit" statt. Sie erinnern an die pompöse Prunkhochzeit von Herzog Georg dem Reichen im Jahr 1475.

The town of Landshut on the banks of the river Isar is about 43 miles north-east of Munich. The good transport links to the capital help the powerful economical performance of the town. A national event which takes place every fourth year is the festival "Landshuter Fürsten-Hochzeit". It replays the grandiose and magnificent marriage of Duke Georg the Rich in 1475.

▲ Die Burg Trausnitz, deren älteste Teile aus dem Jahr 1204 stammen, war ein herzoglicher Sitz.

▲ *Trausnitz castle, of which the oldest part is from about 1204. The castle was a ducal residence.*

◄ Der grüne Inn fließt in die blaue Donau. Der Inn, der von den Alpen kommt, fließt schneller als die Donau und daher drängt das grüne Wasser das blaue beiseite.

◄ *The green river Inn joins the blue Danube. The river Inn which comes down from the alps is faster flowing than the river Danube and therefore the green water pushes the blue water away.*

Passau

Passau

Passau is the easternmost town of Bavaria, close to the Austrian border. The historical city centre, which – thanks to an Italian architect – looks somewhat Mediterranean, is situated on a narrow peninsula where the rivers Inn and Danube join. Not far from this point, the river Ilz joins the Danube, too. This is why Passau is called "town of three rivers". On the top of a small hill is the Baroque cathedral of St. Stephan.

Passau ist die östlichste Stadt Bayerns und liegt direkt an der Grenze zu Österreich. Die dank eines italienischen Baumeisters südländisch anmutende Altstadt liegt auf einer schmalen Halbinsel am Zusammenfluss von Inn und Donau. In der Nähe mündet auch die Ilz in die Donau, weshalb Passau auch „Dreiflüssestadt" genannt wird. Auf einem kleinen Hügel steht der barocke Dom St. Stephan.

Starnberger See
Lake Starnberg

🇩🇪 Im Südwesten vor den Toren Münchens liegt die wohlhabende Stadt Starnberg, von der aus sich der Starnberger See 20 km nach Süden erstreckt. Am nördlichen Ostufer steht beim Schloss Berg ein Holzkreuz im Wasser. Hier ertrank 1886 unter mysteriösen Umständen der bayerische Märchenkönig Ludwig II. Schräg gegenüber, am Westufer, liegt das Schloss Possenhofen, das als „Sissi-Schloss" bekannt wurde.

🇬🇧 *In the south-west of Munich is the town of Starnberg. From here, the lake Starnberg extends 12 miles to the south. On the north-eastern shore is the palace Schloss Berg with a wooden cross standing in the water. This is the point where the Bavarian King Ludwig II mysteriously drowned in the lake in 1886. On the opposite side of the lake is the palace of Possenhofen, known as the Princess Sissy Palace.*

▲ Im Schloss Possenhofen verbrachte die spätere Kaiserin Elisabeth von Österreich („Sissi") ihre Kindheit.

▲ *The palace Possenhofen is the place where the later Empress of Austria, Elisabeth ("Sissi") spent her childhood.*

◄ Der Heimgarten ist ein beliebter und leicht zu besteigender Berg im Tölzer Land.

◄ *The Heimgarten mountain in the Tölz area is very popular and easy to climb.*

Bad Tölz
Bad Tölz

🇬🇧 *30 miles south of Munich is the town of Bad Tölz on the banks of the river Isar. From the early Middle Ages, the densely wooded region provided wood which was transported down the river by numerous raftsmen. In 1476, brewing of beer was started in Tölz. A little later, 22 breweries supplied Munich with beer. In 1846, the largest iodine springs in Germany were discovered, which caused Tölz to develop into a spa.*

🇩🇪 Rund 50 km südlich von München liegt an der Isar die Stadt Bad Tölz. Die waldreiche Umgebung lieferte seit dem frühen Mittelalter Holz, das durch zahlreiche Flößer flussabwärts transportiert wurde. Im Jahr 1476 begann in Tölz die Biersiederei. Bald lieferten 22 Brauereien Bier nach München. Mit der Entdeckung der stärksten Jodquellen Deutschlands im Jahr 1846 entwickelte sich Tölz zum Kurbad.

Berchtesgaden
Berchtesgaden

🔲 Im äußersten Südosten Bayerns liegt Berchtesgaden. Seit dem Mittelalter ist Salz eine wichtige Einnahmequelle der Stadt. Das Salz wird im Bergwerk, das man besichtigen kann, im Wasser gelöst, als „Sole" über Rohrleitungen nach Bad Reichenhall transportiert und dort verarbeitet. Der Königssee mit den Bergen der Watzmanngruppe im Hintergrund ist ein beliebtes und viel fotografiertes Touristenziel.

🇬🇧 *In the very south-east of Bavaria is the town of Berchtesgaden. Since the Middle Ages, salt has been an important source of income for the town. The salt mine is opened to the public. The mineral salt is dissolved in water and then transported by pipeline to the town of Bad Reichenhall for finishing. The lake Königssee with the Watzmann Mountains in the background is an attractive destination for tourists.*

▲ Der Königssee liegt schwer zugänglich zwischen steil aufsteigenden Felswänden. Auf einer kleinen, flachen Landzunge steht seit 1134 die Kirche St. Bartholomä, die zu einem berühmten Wallfahrtsort wurde.

▲ *The lake Königssee is between steep rising mountains and difficult to access. On a small flat spit of land is the church of St. Bartholomä, which was built in 1134 and became a famous place of pilgrimage.*

165

Oberstdorf
Oberstdorf

🔲 Der Kurort Oberstdorf im Allgäu ist die südlichste Gemeinde Deutschlands, von der aus keine Straße weiter nach Süden führt. Österreich ist von hier aus nur über Klettersteige zu erreichen – abgesehen von der österreichischen Enklave „Kleinwalsertal". In und bei Oberstdorf liegen die bekannten alpinen Skigebiete am Nebelhorn, am Fellhorn und an der Kanzelwand, die zu den schneesichersten in Deutschland gehören.

🇬🇧 *The spa Oberstdorf in the Allgäu region is the most southern village of Germany with no road further to the south. Austria can only be reached via mountain paths – apart from the Austrian enclave valley, Kleinwalsertal. Around Oberstdorf are well known skiing areas such as Nebelhorn, Fellhorn and Kanzelwand which are the best assured for snow in Germany.*

◄ Oberstdorf ist nicht zuletzt wegen seiner gewaltigen Skisprungschanze ein bekannter Wintersportort.

◄ *The huge ski-jumping arena is one of the reasons why Oberstdorf is a famous place for winter sports.*

Oberammergau
Oberammergau

Oberammergau liegt etwa 15 km nördlich von Garmisch-Partenkirchen und ist für seine alle zehn Jahre stattfindenden Passionsspiele berühmt. Die Spiele gehen auf ein Gelübde aus dem Pestjahr 1633 zurück. Die aktive Teilnahme als Schauspieler ist für die – ausschließlich Oberammergauer – Bürger eine ehrenvolle Aufgabe und hat Priorität vor den alltäglichen beruflichen Pflichten.

The village of Oberammergau, 10 miles north of Garmisch, is famous for its passion play which takes place every ten years. The event dates back to a vow taken in the year 1633 when the black plague caused havoc. The active participation as a player – exclusively local citizens are allowed – is an honourable duty and has priority over all daily activities of working life.

▲ Die letzten Passionsspiele wurden im Jahr 2000 aufgeführt.

▲ *The last passion play took place in 2000.*

▲ Die Zahnradbahn auf dem Weg zur Zugspitze.

▲ *The rack railway on its way to the Zugspitze.*

Garmisch-Partenkirchen
Garmisch-Partenkirchen

Die selbstständigen Orte Garmisch und Partenkirchen schlossen sich 1935 zusammen, um im Folgejahr gemeinsam die Olympischen Spiele austragen zu können. Partenkirchen war seit der Römerzeit eine Reisestation an einer der wichtigsten Handelsstraßen. Von Garmisch aus führt eine Zahnradbahn auf 2588 m Höhe zur Zugspitze, deren 2962 m hoher Gipfel die höchste Erhebung Deutschlands ist.

The independent villages Garmisch and Partenkirchen fused in 1935 in order to jointly organize the Olympic Games of 1936. Since the Roman era, Partenkirchen was a stop along one of the most important trading routes. From Garmisch, a rack railway leaves for the Zugspitze. The railway station is at an altitude of 8,500 feet, whereas the summit is 9,400 feet high, which is the highest peak in Germany.

Füssen

Füssen

Mit 808 m über Meereshöhe ist Füssen im Allgäu die höchstgelegene Stadt Bayerns. Durch die Stadt fließt der Lech, der im künstlich angelegten Forggensee nördlich von Füssen aufgestaut wird und ein Wasserkraftwerk antreibt. Um 1500 erbauten die Augsburger Fürstbischöfe über der mittelalterlichen Stadt das „Hohe Schloss" als Residenz.

In der Nähe von Füssen, auf dem Gebiet der Gemeinde Schwangau, liegen zwei weitere Schlösser: Das Schloss Hohenschwangau, das vermutlich im 12. Jahrhundert entstand und das der königlichen Familie als Sommerresidenz diente. Nur wenige hundert Meter entfernt davon ließ König Ludwig II. von Bayern 1869 sein romantisches Märchenschloss Neuschwanstein im Stil deutscher Ritterburgen bauen. Der König war ein großer Verehrer Richard Wagners und seiner Opern. Neuschwanstein ist das berühmteste seiner Schlösser und eines der bekanntesten Touristenziele in Deutschland.

At an altitude of 2,650 feet, Füssen in the Allgäu region is the highest town in Bavaria. The river Lech flows through the town and is dammed by the artificial lake Forggensee north of Füssen, where it drives a hydro-electric power station. Around 1500, the Augsburg prince-bishops built their residence "Hohes Schloss" just above the medieval town.

Close to Füssen, on the ground of the town Schwangau, are two more palaces. The palace Hohenschwangau was probably built in the 12th century and served as a summer residence of the royal family. Only a few hundred metres from here, in 1869, King Ludwig II of Bavaria built his romantic palace Neuschwanstein in the style of old German knight's castles. The king was an enthusiastic admirer of Richard Wagner and of his operas. Neuschwanstein is the most famous of his palaces and is one of the best known destinations in Germany.

❚ König Ludwig II. lebte im Schloss Neuschwanstein nur ein halbes Jahr. Als er starb, war erst ein Drittel aller geplanten Räume vollendet.

❚ *King Ludwig II lived only half a year in the palace Neuschwanstein. When he died only one third of all the rooms had been finished.*

Kloster Ettal
Ettal Monastery

In der Nähe von Oberammergau, an der Straße nach Garmisch, wurde im Jahr 1330 das Benediktinerkloster Ettal gegründet. Bei einem Brand 1744 wurden das Kloster und seine Kirche weitgehend zerstört und anschließend im Stil des Hochbarock wieder aufgebaut. Ettal wurde zu einem der bedeutendsten Benediktinerklöster und ist heute mit seiner Brauerei und Destillerie bei Wallfahrern und Touristen ein beliebtes Ziel.

Not far from Oberammergau, at the route to Garmisch is the Benedictine monastery of Ettal, which was founded in 1330. Both the monastery and its church were destroyed by a fire in 1744, but were reconstructed in the style of High Baroque. Ettal developed into one of the most important Benedictine monasteries. Today, with its brewery and its distillery, it is a popular destination for pilgrims and tourists.

► Es ist für den Durchreisenden schwierig, beim Kloster Ettal nicht anzuhalten.

► *It is difficult for the tourist not to make a stop at the Ettal Monastery.*

◄ Die Wieskirche im so genannten Pfaffenwinkel wurde von den berühmten Brüdern Johann Baptist und Dominikus Zimmermann erbaut.

◄ *The church at Wies, located in the so-called "Priest's Corner" was constructed by the famous brothers Johann Baptist and Dominikus Zimmermann.*

Wieskirche
Church Wieskirche

Nordöstlich von Füssen, auf dem Gebiet der Gemeinde Steingaden, steht in der freien Natur eine der berühmtesten Wallfahrtskirchen, die Wieskirche. Die in den Jahren 1745 bis 1754 erbaute Rokokokirche sollte im 19. Jahrhundert im Zuge der Säkularisation abgerissen werden, wurde aber von den einheimischen Bauern gerettet. Heute besuchen jährlich über eine Million Menschen die Kirche.

North-east of Füssen, on the territory of the village Steingaden, in the open countryside, is one of the most famous pilgrimage churches: Wieskirche. The Rococo style church was built from 1745 to 1754 and was to be pulled down during the secularization in the 19th century. However, local farmers saved the church. Today, millions of guests visit the church.

Schloss Linderhof
Palace Linderhof

▬ In einem Seitental bei Oberammergau ließ König Ludwig II. von 1874 bis 1878 eine „königliche Villa" bauen, das Schloss Linderhof. Es ist das kleinste der Schlösser Ludwigs und das einzige, das zu seinen Lebzeiten vollendet wurde. Ursprünglich stand an dieser Stelle ein Jagdhäuschen seines Vaters Maximilian II., das Ludwig um 200 m versetzen ließ, wo es heute noch steht.

Gleichzeitig mit dem Bau des Schlosses wurden die Parkanlagen errichtet. Es entstanden unter anderem eine Terrassenanlage mit einem kleinen Venustempel, ein großes Wasserbecken mit einer 22 m hohen Fontäne und ein Musikpavillon.

Das Schloss verfügt über ein Tischleindeckdich: Der Tisch des Speisesaals kann durch eine Mechanik nach unten in die Küche abgesenkt, dort gedeckt und wieder nach oben gekurbelt werden. König Ludwig II. verbrachte im Schloss Linderhof mehr Zeit als in allen anderen Schlössern.

🇬🇧 *In a small valley near Oberammergau King Ludwig II built a "royal villa" from 1874 to 1878, the palace Linderhof. It is the smallest of all his palaces and it is the only one which was finished before he died. At first, at this place there was a hunting lodge of his father Maximilian II, which then was shifted by 200 metres, where it is still today.*

At the same time the garden was built, including terraces, a small Venus temple and a large pool with a 72-foot-high fountain and a music pavilion.

The palace has a funny table, the so-called Tischleindeckdich: A mechanical mechanism allows lowering the table of the dining room down into the kitchen, where it is set and then lifted back into the dining room. King Ludwig II spent more time in Linderhof than in any other palace.

❼ Das Schloss Linderhof war ein beliebter Aufenthaltsort des Königs Ludwig II. Es wurde als einziges Schloss noch zu seinen Lebzeiten vollendet.

❼ *The Palace Linderhof was a favourite place of king Ludwig II. It is the only palace which was finished before he died.*

169

Bad Wörishofen
Bad Wörishofen

▬ Bad Wörishofen ist ein bekannter Kurort etwa in der Mitte zwischen Augsburg und Füssen und rund 90 km westlich von München. Um das Jahr 1889 begann hier der Kurbetrieb unter der Leitung des Pfarrers Sebastian Kneipp, dem Begründer der nach ihm benannten Wasserkuren. Kneipp war 1849 an der Tuberkulose hoffnungslos erkrankt, als er ein Buch über die Heilkraft des frischen Wassers entdeckte.

🇬🇧 *The town of Bad Wörishofen is a well known spa about 56 miles west of Munich, half-way between Augsburg and Füssen. In about 1889, health cures were started under the leadership of parish priest Sebastian Kneipp, the founder of the water based cures named after him. Kneipp himself had fallen hopelessly ill with tuberculosis, when he discovered a book about the healing power of fresh water.*

▲ Die moderne, neue Therme Bad Wörishofen

▲ *The new modern thermal spa, Bad Wörishofen*

170

◄ Das Schwarze Moor in der Bayerischen Rhön ist eines der bedeutendsten Moore in Mitteleuropa.

◄ *The Black Moor in the Bavarian Rhön is one of the most significant moors in Central Europe.*

Rhön
Rhön

🇬🇧 *The Rhön is a low mountain range in the border area of the states Bavaria, Hesse and Thuringia. The highest summits are close to 3,000 feet high. In the Middle Ages, the Rhön was an important supplier of beech wood. Here and there, the primeval forests still exist and form the core of the Biosphere Reserve Rhön. The higher regions are home to a number of rare types of plants.*

▬ Die Rhön ist ein Mittelgebirge im Grenzgebiet der Bundesländer Bayern, Hessen und Thüringen. Die höchsten Berge erreichen Höhen von über 900 m. Im Mittelalter war die Rhön ein wichtiger Lieferant von Buchenholz. Teilweise bestehen die Wälder noch in ihrer Urform und sind als Kernzonen im Biosphärenreservat Rhön ausgewiesen. In den Hochlagen kommen verschiedene seltene Pflanzenarten vor.

Spessart
Spessart

▬ Der Spessart liegt als Mittelgebirge mit flachen Kuppen im nordwestlichen Bayern und grenzt nach Süden hin an den Main an. Seinen Namen verdankt der Spessart („Spechtswald") dem Schwarzspecht, der das Symboltier der Region ist. Der Spessart war lange Zeit politisch zersplittert und wurde erst sehr spät besiedelt. Die mittelalterlichen Geschichten über Räuberbanden im Spessart haben einen realen Hintergrund.

🇬🇧 *The Spessart is a relatively flat low mountain range in the north-west of Bavaria. In the south, it borders the river Main. The name Spessart is derived from the black woodpecker (German: "Specht"), which is the symbolic animal of the region. For a long time, the Spessart was politically fragmented and was settled very late. The medieval stories about robber bands in the Spessart do have a real background.*

► Das Wasserschloss Mespelbrunn war einer der Drehorte des Spielfilms „Das Wirtshaus im Spessart".

► *The moated castle Mespelbrunn is a place where the movie "Das Wirtshaus im Spessart" was produced.*

171

◄ Der Geigenbau prägt immer noch das Leben in Mittenwald.

◄ *Manufacturing of string instruments still dominates life in Mittenwald.*

Mittenwald
Mittenwald

🇬🇧 *The way from Garmisch to Innsbruck – just before it crosses the border to Austria – leads through Mittenwald in the upper valley of the river Isar. In the Middle Ages, the village was an important trade centre on the route to Venice. Since 1685, the tradition of violin-making had developed in Mittenwald. Alongside Neunkirchen in Saxony, Mittenwald is the most significant centre of string instruments.*

▬ Auf dem Weg von Garmisch nach Innsbruck passiert man kurz vor der Grenze nach Österreich die Gemeinde Mittenwald im oberen Isartal. Im Mittelalter war der Ort ein bedeutender Umschlagplatz auf der Handelsroute nach Venedig. Seit 1685 hat sich in Mittenwald die Geigenbautradition entwickelt. Mittenwald ist neben Markneukirchen in Sachsen das bedeutendste Zentrum für Streich- und Zupfinstrumente.

Coburg
Coburg

▬ Im Norden Bayerns, an der Grenze zu Thüringen, liegt Coburg, die ehemalige Residenzstadt der Herzöge von Sachsen-Coburg. Coburg schloss sich sehr frühzeitig der Reformation an und nahm 1530 Martin Luther auf. Der Komponist Johann Strauß wurde Coburger Bürger, um 1887 seine evangelische Braut heiraten zu können. Seit 1992 findet in Coburg jedes Jahr das größte Samba-Festival außerhalb Brasiliens statt.

▲ Der Marktplatz von Coburg mit Rathaus und Prinz-Albert-Denkmal

🇬🇧 *In the north of Bavaria, next to Thuringia, is Coburg, the former residence city of the Dukes of Saxe-Coburg. The town followed the Reformation quite early and took in Martin Luther in 1530. The composer Johann Strauß became a Coburg citizen in order to be allowed to marry his Protestant bride. Every year since 1992, the largest Samba festival outside Brazil is held in Coburg.*

▲ *The market place of Coburg with the town hall and the Prince Albert Monument*

172

Fichtelgebirge
Fichtelgebirge

▬ Das Fichtelgebirge liegt im Nordosten Bayerns, östlich bis nordöstlich von Bayreuth. Die höchsten Gipfel sind der Schneeberg mit 1053 m und der Ochsenkopf mit 1024 m. Vom frühen Mittelalter bis zum Dreißigjährigen Krieg wurden im Fichtelgebirge Gold, Zinn und Eisen abgebaut. Heute ist im Fichtelgebirge mit der Stadt Selb das Zentrum der deutschen Porzellanindustrie beheimatet.

🇬🇧 *The low mountain area Fichtelgebirge is in the north-east of Bavaria, east to north-east of Bayreuth. The highest peaks are the 3,455-foot-high Schneeberg and the 3,360-foot-high Ochsenkopf. From the early Middle Ages until the Thirty Years' War, gold, tin and iron ore were mined in the region. Today, the Fichtelgebirge town of Selb is the centre of the German china industry.*

◄ In der Nähe der Stadt Wunsiedel befindet sich die Luisenburg mit dem so genannten Felsenlabyrinth.

◄ *Not far from the town of Wunsiedel ist the castle Luisenburg with the so-called rock labyrinth.*

Bayerischer Wald
Bavarian Forest

◾ Der Bayerische Wald ist ein Mittelgebirge im Osten des Landes. Der Gebirgszug setzt sich hinter der tschechischen Grenze fort, wird aber dann Böhmerwald genannt. Insgesamt handelt es sich um eines der größten Waldgebiete in Europa. Die höchsten Berge des Bayerischen Waldes, der Große Arber und der Rachel, sind 1456 bzw. 1453 m hoch.

Der Nationalpark Bayerischer Wald ist der älteste in Deutschland und umfasst heute 240 km². Der Park umfasst einige Gebiete mit urwaldähnlichem Bewuchs sowie kleine Seen und Moore. Am Fuß des Großen Falkenstein befinden sich weitläufige Freigehege, in denen mit etwas Glück Bären, Luchse, Wölfe, Wildschweine, Wildpferde und Urrinder beobachtet werden können.

Durch den Bayerischen Wald verläuft die „Glasstraße", an der historische Glashütten und bekannte Orte der Glasbläserkunst liegen, insbesondere Bodenmais, Zwiesel, Frauenau, Spiegelau und Grafenau.

🇬🇧 *The Bavarian Forest is a low mountain range in the east of the state. It expands beyond the border to the Czech Republic, but is then named Bohemian Forest. Altogether, it is one of the largest forest regions in Europe. The highest mountains of the Bavarian Forest are Großer Arber (4,780 feet) and Rachel (4,770 feet).*

The 93 sq mile National Park Bavarian Forest is the oldest one in Germany. The park has some areas of primeval like forest as well as a number of small lakes and moors. At the foot of the mountain Großer Falkenstein, there is a widespread outdoor enclosure, where – with good luck – bears, lynx, wolfs, wild pigs, wild horses and aurochs can be watched.

A popular route through the Bavarian Forest is the "Glasstraße" which connects historical glassworks with well known glass-blower towns, especially Bodenmais, Zwiesel, Frauenau, Spiegelau and Grafenau.

❚ Der Gipfel des Großen Rachel an der Grenze zu Tschechien ist ein beliebtes Ziel der Wanderer. Bei gutem Wetter reicht der Blick bis zu den Alpen.

❚ *The summit of the Großer Rachel near the border with the Czech Republic is a favourite goal for hikers. In good weather conditions the alps can be seen.*

▲ Das Wahrzeichen der Stadt Lindau ist
die Hafeneinfahrt mit dem Leuchtturm
und dem Bayerischen Löwen, deren
momentaner Eigentümer allerdings die
Stadt Konstanz ist.

▲ *The symbol of the town of Lindau is the*
port entrance with its lighthouse and the
Bavarian lion, the current owner of
which, however, is the town of Constance.

Bodensee
Lake Constance

🇬🇧 *Lake Constance is the largest German lake,*
although it is shared with Switzerland and Austria.
It is almost 40 miles long and between the German
town of Friedrichshafen and the Swiss town of
Romanshorn almost 9 miles wide. Because of the
earth's curvature, it is not possible to see the opposite
shore in the longitudinal direction at ground level.

The oldest known settlements on the shore of the
lake are from the recent Stone Age, which was
4,000 to 5,000 years ago. The reconstructed build-
ings on stilts near the village of Unteruhldingen –
between Meersburg and Überlingen – were such
a settlement.

Out of the total shore length of Lake Constance,
only 12 miles are Bavarian. Within this area is the
town of Lindau. The historical town centre is on an
island and is connected with the mainland via both
a railway dam and a bridge. The largest fruit grow-
ing region of Germany expands from Lindau along
the shore of the lake. About 250,000 metric tons of
apples ("Bodenseeäpfel") are produced every year,
furthermore cherries, pears and grapes.

▬ Der Bodensee ist der größte deutsche See, den sich Deutschland allerdings mit der Schweiz und mit Österreich teilt. Die
Gesamtlänge beträgt fast 64 km und die größte Breite zwischen
Friedrichshafen und Romanshorn 14 km. Aufgrund der Erdkrüm-
mung ist es nicht möglich, dass man aus menschlicher Perspek-
tive das in Längsrichtung gegenüberliegende Ufer, zum Beispiel
Lindau oder Konstanz, sehen kann.

Die ältesten bekannten Siedlungen am Ufer des Bodensees stam-
men aus der Jungsteinzeit, sind also 4000 bis 5000 Jahre alt.
Die rekonstruierten Pfahlbauten bei Unteruhldingen – zwischen
Meersburg und Überlingen – waren eine solche Siedlung.

Von der gesamten Uferlänge des Bodensees entfallen auf Bayern
19 km. Auf bayerischem Gebiet liegt die Stadt Lindau. Die historische Altstadt liegt auf einer Insel und ist durch einen Eisenbahn-
damm und eine Brücke mit dem Festland verbunden. Von Lindau
an erstreckt sich entlang des Bodensees die größte Obstregion
Deutschlands. Jährlich werden etwa 250 000 Tonnen Bodenseeäpfel produziert, ferner Kirschen, Birnen und Wein.

Ammersee
Lake Ammersee

■ Etwa 50 km westlich von München liegt der drittgrößte bayerische See. Er hat eine Fläche von 47 km² und
eine maximale Tiefe von 80 m. Der Ammersee ist ein außerordentlich beliebtes Segelrevier. Die private Nutzung
durch Motorboote ist dagegen im Sinne des Naturschutzes
sehr stark eingeschränkt. Auf dem „heiligen Berg" oberhalb von Herrsching am Ostufer befindet sich das bekannte Kloster Andechs.

🇬🇧 *About 30 miles west of Munich is the third largest
Bavarian lake, the 18 sq-mile-large Ammersee. Its depth
is up to 260 feet. The lake is an extremely popular sailing
area. The private usage of motor boats however, is extremely limited for reasons of nature conservancy. On the top
of the so-called holy hill above Herrsching, on the eastern
shore of the lake, is the well known monastery Andechs.*

► Segeln am Ammersee bei Sonnenuntergang

► *Sailing on the lake Ammersee at sunset*

175

Tegernsee
Lake Tegernsee

■ Der Tegernsee südlich von München ist nicht nur ein
beliebtes Naherholungsziel, sondern auch ein bedeutendes Urlaubsgebiet. Rund um den See liegen mehrere
sehenswerte Ortschaften, darunter die Stadt Tegernsee
mit dem ehemaligen Benediktinerkloster und späteren
königlichen Schloss, das elegante Rottach-Egern mit
seiner Spitzengastronomie und der Kurort Bad Wiessee
mit seinem Spielkasino.

🇬🇧 *The lake Tegernsee south of Munich is not only a popular recreational area but also an important holiday region.
Around the lake are some towns worth seeing. Among
them is the town of Tegernsee with its royal palace which
was formerly a Benedictine monastery, furthermore the
elegant town of Rottach-Egern with its top gastronomy and
the spa Bad Wiessee with its gambling casino.*

◄ Ballonfahrten über dem winterlichen Tegernsee gehören zu den
touristischen Attraktionen der Region.

◄ *Balloon rides in wintertime across the lake Tegernsee are part of
the touristic attraction of that region.*

Chiemsee
Lake Chiemsee

Der Chiemsee ist mit 80 km² Fläche der größte bayerische See. Er entstand am Ende der letzten Eiszeit vor rund 10 000 Jahren. Die Landschaft um den Chiemsee, der Chiemgau, ist eines der beliebtesten Erholungsgebiete Bayerns. Der See ist ein sehr beliebtes Segelrevier. Bekannt ist der See vor allem durch zwei seiner Inseln. Die 15,5 ha große Insel Frauenchiemsee mit dem Kloster Frauenwörth ist ein Wallfahrtsort. Auf der Insel leben etwa 200 Einwohner.

Die weitaus größere Insel, Herrenchiemsee, hat eine Fläche von 238 ha. Sie ist fast unbewohnt, bietet jedoch eine herausragende Touristenattraktion. Hier ließ der bayerische „Märchenkönig" Ludwig II. ein Schloss im Stil des Schlosses von Versailles bauen. Das „Neue Schloss Herrenchiemsee" wurde nie fertiggestellt und Ludwig II. wohnte insgesamt nur wenige Tage hier. Während der Bauphase hielt er sich gelegentlich im Alten Schloss Herrenchiemsee, einem ehemaligen Kloster, auf.

❚ Das Schloss von Versailles war Vorbild, als König Ludwig II. das Schloss Herrenchiemsee bauen ließ. Eine Reihe von Details, die in Versailles längst zerstört waren, wurden in Herrenchiemsee rekonstruiert.

❚ The palace of Versailles was the model when King Ludwig II built the palace Herrenchiemsee. A number of details which had already been destroyed in Versailles were rebuilt in Herrenchiemsee.

With an area of 260 sq miles the Chiemsee is the largest Bavarian lake. It was formed at the end of the most recent ice age about 10,000 years ago. The region around the lake, the so-called Chiemgau, is one of the most popular recreation areas in Bavaria. The lake is a real paradise for sailors. And it is well known for two islands: The 38-acre-large island Frauenchiemsee with its cloister Frauenwörth is a pilgrim's destination. About 200 people are living on the island.

The much larger island is the 588-acre Herrenchiemsee, which is not populated but offers an extraordinary tourist attraction. The Bavarian King Ludwig II ordered the building of a palace there in the style of the palace of Versailles. This "Neue Schloss Herrenchiemsee" has never been completely finished. Ludwig II lived here only a few days. During the time of construction he sometimes lived in the old palace, which is a former monastery.

Kloster Weltenburg
Weltenburg Monastery

🟦 Das Kloster Weltenburg, das um 617 von Wandermönchen gegründet wurde, liegt in der Nähe der Stadt Kehlheim an der Donau und ist das älteste Kloster in Bayern. Seine Brauerei, die älteste Klosterbrauerei der Welt, produziert seit dem Jahr 1050 Bier. Im Jahr 2004 erhielt das „Weltenburger Kloster Barock Dunkel" als bestes Dunkelbier den „World Beer Award". Ein Problem stellt das häufig auftretende Hochwasser der Donau dar.

◄ Das Kloster liegt an einer Stelle, wo sich die Donau vor 130 000 Jahren einen neuen Weg durch die Felsen gebahnt hat.

◄ *The monastery is located at a place where 130,000 years ago the river Danube found a new way through te rocks.*

🇬🇧 *The monastery of Weltenburg which was founded by travelling monks in about 617 is close to the town of Kehlheim on the banks of the river Danube. It is the oldest monastery of Bavaria. Its brewery, the oldest of the world, has produced beer since 1050. In 2004, the label "Weltenburger Kloster Barock Dunkel" received the "World Beer Award" as the best dark beer. A major problem is the frequent flooding of the Danube.*

Kochelsee/Walchensee
Lake Kochelsee/ Lake Walchensee

🟦 Etwa 70 km südlich von München befinden sich der Kochelsee und der 200 m höher gelegene Walchensee. Die großartige Landschaft zog viele berühmte Maler an, darunter Franz Marc und die Künstlergruppe „Blaue Reiter". Im Jahr 1924 wurde das Walchenseekraftwerk in Betrieb genommen, das bis heute eines der größten Kraftwerke seiner Art ist. In Rohrleitungen stürzt das Wasser vom Walchensee zum Kochelsee, wo es die Turbinen antreibt.

🇬🇧 *About 43 miles south of Munich are the lakes Kochelsee and – 660 feet higher in altitude – Walchensee. The great landscape attracted many famous artists; among them Franz Marc and the artist group "The Blue Rider". In 1924, the Walchensee power station was started up, which is one of the largest hydroelectric power stations of this kind until now. The water from the lake Walchensee streams down in pipes to Kochelsee where it drives the engines.*

► Der Walchensee ist einer der wenigen noch unberührten Seen in den bayerischen Alpen.

► *The lake Walchensee is one of the very few unspoiled lakes in the Bavarian Alps.*

Register
Index

Aachen 86
Ammersee 175
Arnstadt 109
Augsburg 162
Bad Hersfeld 121
Bad Tölz 164
Bad Wörishofen 170
Baden-Baden 149
Baden-Württemberg 144–153
Bamberg 159
Bautzen 102
Bayern 154–177
Bayreuth 158
Bayerischer Wald 173
Berchtesgaden 165
Bergisches Land 90
Berlin 60–73
Berliner Dom 67
Binnen- und Außenalster 31
Bodensee 174
Bonn 87
Brandenburg 40–49
Bremen 36–37
Bremerhaven 38
Burg Querfurt 81
Celle 53
Chemnitz 98
Chiemsee 176
Coburg 172
Cottbus 44
Cuxhaven 59
Darmstadt 117
Dessau 77
Deutsche Alleenstraße 24
Deutsche Weinstraße 135
Dresden 94–95
Düsseldorf 84–85
Eifel 91
Eisenach 108
Elbsandsteingebirge 101
Emsland 56
Erfurt 106–107
Erzgebirge 103
Essen 85
Fichtelgebirge 172
Fischmarkt 33
Flensburg 15
Frankfurt 119
Frankfurt a. d. Oder 45

Freiburg 151
Freie Hansestadt Bremen 34–39
Friedrichstraße 73
Funkturm 66
Füssen 167
Garmisch-Partenkirchen 166
Gartenreich Dessau-Wörlitz 80
Gedächtniskirche 65
Gendarmenmarkt 71
Gera 111
Gießen 121
Glashütte 100
Gotha 107
Göttingen 54
Halle 78
Hamburg 28–33
Hamburger Hafen 32
Hameln 54
Hannover 52–53
Harz 57
Havel 49
Heidelberg 148
Heilbronn 148
Hessen 114–125
Holsteinische Schweiz 17
Idar-Oberstein 131
Industrie 143
Ingolstadt 162
Insel Amrum 14
Insel Hiddensee 23
Insel Mainau 152
Insel Rügen 24
Insel Sylt 14
Insel Usedom 25
Jena 112
KaDeWe 73
Kaiserslautern 135
Karlsruhe 149
Kassel 125
Kiel 12–13
Kloster Ettal 168
Kloster Weltenburg 177
Koblenz 131
Kochelsee/Walchensee 177
Köln 86
Konstanz 151
Kurfürstendamm 68
Lahn 124

Landshut 163
Leipzig 96
Lübeck 16
Ludwigshafen 133
Lüneburg 56
Lüneburger Heide 57
Magdeburg 76–77
Main 124
Mainz 128–129
Marburg 120
Mecklenburg-Vorpommern 18–27
Meiningen 109
Meißen 97
Mittellandkanal 81
Mittenwald 171
Mosel 137
München 156–157
Münsterland 89
Müritz 27
Museumsinsel 70
Neubrandenburg 26
Neunkirchen 142
Niedersachsen 50–59
Nikolaiviertel 71
Nordrhein-Westfalen 82–91
Nürburgring 135–134
Nürnberg 160
Oberammergau 166
Oberstdorf 165
Odenwald 122
Oldenburg 55
Olympiastadion 72
Osnabrück 55
Ostfriesische Inseln 58
Passau 163
Pforzheim 147
Potsdam 42–43
Potsdamer Platz 69
Quedlinburg 79
Radebeul 101
Ravensburg 152
Regensburg 160
Rhein 136
Rheinland-Pfalz 126–137
Rhön 170
Rostock 22
Rothenburg o. T. 161
Rüdesheim 118
Ruhrgebiet 88

Saar 142
Saarbrücken 140–141
Saarland 138–143
Saarlouis 141
Sachsen 92–103
Sachsen-Anhalt 74–81
Sächsisches Vogtland 102
Sauerland 90
Schleswig-Holstein 10–17
Schloss Bellevue 65
Schloss Cecilienhof 46
Schloss Charlottenburg 64
Schloss Linderhof 169
Schloss Sanssouci 47
Schwäbische Alb 153
Schwarzwald 153
Schwerin 20
Siegerland 91
Siegessäule 66
Spessart 171
Speyer 132
Spree und Spreewald 48
St. Pauli 33
Starnberger See 164
Stralsund 23
Stuttgart 146–147
Taunus 123
Tegernsee 175
Teutoburger Wald 89
Thüringen 104–113
Thüringer Wald 113
Trier 130
Tübingen 150
Uckermark 49
Ulm 150
Unter den Linden 69
Weimar 110
Wernigerode 79
Weser 39
Wetzlar 118
Wiesbaden 116–117
Wieskirche 168
Wismar 21
Wittenberg 78
Worms 132
Würzburg 159
Zittau 98
Zwickau 99

Aachen	86	Friedrichstraße	73
Amrum Island	14	Füssen	167
Arnstadt	109	Garmisch-Partenkirchen	166
Augsburg	162	Gedächtniskirche	65
Bad Hersfeld	121	Gendarmenmarkt	71
Bad Tölz	164	Gera	111
Bad Wörishofen	170	German Avenue Route	24
Baden-Baden	149	German Wine Route	135
Baden-Wurttemberg	144–153	Gießen	121
Bamberg	159	Glashütte	100
Bautzen	102	Gotha	107
Bavaria	154–177	Göttingen	54
Bavarian Forest	173	Halle	78
Bayreuth	158	Hamburg	28–33
Berchtesgaden	165	Hamelin	54
Bergisches Land	90	Hanover	52–53
Berlin	60–73	Harz	57
Berlin Cathedral	67	Heidelberg	148
Bonn	87	Heilbronn	148
Brandenburg	40–49	Hesse	114–125
Bremen	36–37	Hiddensee Island	23
Bremerhaven	38	Holstein's Switzerland	17
Celle	53	Idar-Oberstein	131
Chemnitz	98	Industrie	143
Church Wieskirche	168	Ingolstadt	162
Coburg	172	Island of Rügen	24
Cologne	86	Jena	112
Constance	151	KaDeWe	73
Cottbus	44	Kaiserslautern	135
Cuxhaven	59	Karlsruhe	149
Darmstadt	117	Kassel	125
Dessau	77	Kiel	12–13
Dresden	94–95	Koblenz	131
Düsseldorf	84–85	Kurfürstendamm	68
East Frisian Islands	58	Lake Ammersee	175
Eifel	91	Lake Chiemsee	176
Eisenach	108	Lake Constance	174
Elbe Sandstone		Lake Kochelsee/	
Mountains	101	Lake Walchensee	177
Emsland	56	Lake Müritz	27
Erfurt	106–107	Lake Starnberg	164
Essen	85	Lake Tegernsee	175
Fichtelgebirge	172	Lakes Binnen- and	
Fish Market	33	Außenalster	31
Flensburg	15	Landshut	163
Frankfurt	119	Leipzig	96
Frankfurt a. d. Oder	45	Lower Saxony	50–59
Free Hanseatic City of		Lübeck	16
Bremen	34–39	Ludwigshafen	133
Freiburg	151	Lüneburg	56

Lüneburger Heide	57	River Weser	39
Magdeburg	76–77	Rostock	22
Mainau Island	152	Rothenburg o. T.	161
Mainz	128–129	Rüdesheim	118
Marburg	120	Ruhr Area	88
Mecklenburg-Lower		Saarbrücken	140–141
Pomerania	18–27	Saarland	138–143
Meiningen	109	Saarlouis	141
Meißen	97	Sauerland	90
Midland Canal	81	Saxon Vogtland	102
Mittenwald	171	Saxony	92–103
Monastery Ettal	168	Saxony-Anhalt	74–81
Monastery Weltenburg	177	Schleswig-Holstein	10–17
Munich	156–157	Schloss Bellevue	65
Münsterland	89	Schloss Cecilienhof	46
Museum Island	70	Schloss Charlottenburg	64
Neubrandenburg	26	Schloss Sanssouci	47
Neunkirchen	142	Schwarzwald	153
Nikolaiviertel	71	Schwerin	20
North Rhine-Westphalia	82–91	Siegerland	91
Nuremberg	160	Spessart	171
Nürburgring	134	Speyer	132
Oberammergau	166	St. Pauli	33
Oberstdorf	165	Stralsund	23
Odenwald	122	Stuttgart	146–147
Oldenburg	55	Sylt Island	14
Olympic Stadium	72	Taunus	123
Ore Mountains	103	Teutoburg Forest	89
Osnabrück	55	The Port of Hamburg	32
Palace Linderhof	169	The Swabian Jura	153
Passau	163	Thuringia	104–113
Pforzheim	147	Thuringian Forest	113
Potsdam	42–43	Trier	130
Potsdamer Platz	69	Triumphal Column	66
Quedlinburg	79	Tübingen	150
Querfurt Castle	81	Uckermark	49
Radebeul	101	Ulm	150
Radio Tower Berlin	66	Unter den Linden	69
Ravensburg	152	Usedom Island	25
Regensburg	160	Weimar	110
Rhineland-Palatinate	126–137	Wernigerode	79
Rhön	170	Wetzlar	118
River Havel	49	Wiesbaden	116–117
River Lahn	124	Wismar	21
River Main	124	Wittenberg	78
River Moselle	137	Wörlitz Park	80
River Rhine	136	Worms	132
River Saar	142	Würzburg	159
River Spree and		Zittau	98
the Spreewald	48	Zwickau	99

Bildnachweis

Wir danken folgenden Firmen und Personen für ihre freundliche
Unterstützung:

Archiv Tourist-Information Coburg 172 (o)
August Horch Museum Zwickau 99
Bayerische Zugspitzbahn, Bergbahn AG Garmisch-Partenkirchen 166 (u)
Bayern Tourismus Marketing GmbH, www.bayern.by 156 (u), 158–159,
    160 (u), 162 (o), 163 (o), 163 (u), 164 (u), 166 (o), 176–177 (o), 177 (u)
BIS Büro Bremerhaven-Werbung 34–35, 38
Chemnitz Tourismus 98 (o)
christian andreas müller – fuenfseenland.de 164 (o)
CMT Cottbus GmbH 44
Copyright Stuttgart-Marketing GmbH 146 (u)
Emsland Touristik GmbH 56 (u)
Festspielstadt Wunsiedel 172 (u)
Foto: Lothar Sprenger, Copyright Meissen® 97
Foto: Lutz Ebhardt 107 (u)
Foto: Thorsten Ritzmann 55 (u)
Gera Tourismus e. V./Foto: Schuck 111 (u)
Glashütte Original 100
Infozentrum Rhön 170 (u)
Ingolstadt Tourismus und Kongress GmbH 162 (u)
Investitions- und Marketinggesellschaft Sachsen-Anhalt mbH/
    Foto: Hans-Wulf Kunze 79 (u)
    Foto: M. Fechner 81 (u)
    Foto: Thomas Ziegler 78 (o)
Kongress- und Touristik Service Region Saarbrücken GmbH 140 (u)
Kurdirektion Bad Wörishofen 170 (o)
Magdeburg Marketing Kongress und Tourismus GmbH 76–77 (o), 76 (u)
Nürburgring GmbH/Thomas Urner 134 (u)
OMT, Foto: Detlef Heese 55 (o)
Presseamt Stadt Bonn/Foto: Michael Sondermann 87
RPT-Tourismus GmbH/
    © Ahr Rhein Eifel Tourismus & Service GmbH 135 (u)
    Stadt Speyer, Foto: Thorsten Krüger 132 (u)
    © Stadtarchiv Worms 132 (o)
    © Tourist Information Kaiserslautern 134–135 (o)
Rüdesheimer Seilbahngesellschaft 118 (o)
Sauerland-Tourismus e. V. 90 (u)
Spielbank Wiesbaden GmbH & Co. KG 116–117 (o)
Stadt Meiningen 109 (u)
Stadt Pforzheim 147 (u)
Stadt Ravensburg 152 (o)
Stadtentwicklungsgesellschaft Neubrandenburg mbH 26
Stadtmarketing Arnstadt GmbH 109 (o)
Stadtverwaltung Querfurt M. Kaulfuß 80–81 (o)
Taunus Touristik Service e. V. 123
Tourismus Gesellschaft Erfurt/Foto: Barbara Neumann 106 (u)
Tourismus Marketing Gesellschaft Sachsen mbH 102 (u)
Tourismus Marketing Niedersachsen GmbH 52–53 (o), 53 (u), 56–57 (o),
    57 (u), 58 (u), 59 (o)
Tourismus und Sport Oberstdorf 165 (u)
Tourismus Zentrale Saarland GmbH 138–139, 141 (u)
Tourismus-Marketing GmbH Baden-Württemberg 148 (u), 151 (o),
    153 (o, kl. Bild)
Tourismus-Marketing GmbH Baden-Württemberg/
    Foto: Achim Mende 151 (u)
Tourismusverband Ammersee-Lech e. V. 175 (o)
Tourismusverein Frankfurt (Oder) e. V. 45
Tourist-Info Zittau/Foto: Rene Pech 98 (u)
Tourist-Information Bad Hersfeld e. V. 121 (u)
Tourist-Information Gießen/Foto: Rolf Wegst 121 (o)
Tourist-Information Idar-Oberstein 131 (u)
Tourist-Information Mittenwald 171 (u)
Uckermark (tmu GmbH) 49 (u)
Universität Göttingen – Pressestelle 54 (o)
Weltkulturerbe Völklinger Hütte/Gerhard Kassner 142 (o)
Wilhelm-Hack-Museum 133

Alle weiteren Fotos: SAMMÜLLER KREATIV GmbH